HOW JESUS WON PERSONS

D1016033

225

HOW JESUS WON PERSONS

DELOS MILES

BROADMAN PRESS
Nashville, Tennessee

4262-36
ISBN: 0-8054-6236-8

Dewey Decimal Classification: 232.95
Subject Heading: JESUS CHRIST—PUBLIC MINISTRY // EVANGELISTIC WORK

Library of Congress Catalog Card Number: 82-70049
Printed in the United States of America

Dedicated to the memory
of L. R. Scarborough and Gaines S. Dobbins,
two pioneer teachers of
evangelism who were captivated
by the great truth that Jesus
Christ alone is the perfect model
for evangelism

Contents

Introduction

I offer these fifteen case studies in the evangelism of Jesus as a natural sequel to my *Master Principles of Evangelism*.[1] They are designed for the use of rank and file pastors and lay leaders in the churches.

If you and I want to learn how to more effectively win persons to Christ, let us study how Jesus dealt with individuals, groups, and structures. Jesus was the master witness. He is our perfect model for witnessing.

Leighton Ford commenting on personal evangelism says, "Thirty-five interviews of Jesus . . . are recorded in the Gospels."[2] Each of those interviews is worthy of our most careful and detailed study. This volume is an attempt to examine fifteen of those personal witnessing encounters in the life and ministry of our Lord.

Some readers will be familiar with the modern case study techniques which are enjoying enthusiastic acceptance in the study of a number of subjects including business administration, missions, and evangelism. While some of those techniques may be applied with profit to the study of New Testament cases in personal evangelism, I caution against superimposing such analytical methods upon an inspired text which was revealed in very different cultures than our own.

My approach in each case is to try to answer the question: "What lessons may we learn from this case which may be applied to our evangelism?" I do use some contemporary cases and illustrations from our time and culture to apply those lessons from these very special, first-century cases in Palestine. As a matter of fact, I have a burning desire to relate much of what has been written on personal evangelism during the past five to seven years to these fifteen pattern-type cases. Particularly do I hope to demonstrate how the evangelizing of Jesus illuminates what has been variously called friendship, household, *oikos,* relational, life-style, incarnational, service, web, affirmation, and inductive evangelism.

Herschel H. Hobbs calls some of these cases the "wayside ministry" of Jesus. Examples which he cites are the cases of Bartimaeus (Mark 10:46-52), the Gerasene demoniac (Luke 8:26-39), the man blind from birth (John 9:1 *ff.*), the woman taken in adultery (John 8:1 *ff.*), and especially the woman of Samaria (John 4:3 *ff.*).[3] You will note that I treat three of those five cases. Some see these as chance meetings with those who needed him. I prefer to view them as providential and divine appointments.

The reader is entitled to know that I believe Jesus Christ, as he is revealed in the Bible, to be the norm for judging and shaping all evangelization. I doubt that we shall ever encounter a greater or more useful idea in evangelism than that Jesus of Nazareth was, and is, and ever shall be the only perfect model evangelist.

Finally, some of the lessons which I lift up are emphasized in more than one of the cases. If such overlapping needs justification, consider this. One holiday season I sat through a three-hour performance of George Frederic Handel's *Messiah.* It was a highlight of my Christmas that year. A point which struck me about the oratorio was the continuous use of repetition. Especially noticeable was the repetition of those early verses from Isaiah 53 at the beginning of part 2. The counter tenor kept repeating the text of Isaiah 53:3 and 50:6, whereas the choir kept repeating Isaiah 53:4-6. Together, with the orchestra, they drove those words forever into my mind.[4]

I am more convinced than ever that one of the ways we learn is through repetition. Therefore, whatever repetition there is in this volume, I hope it will help to fix forever these lessons in your mind and heart.

The end notes on each chapter will reveal some of my indebtedness to a variety of sources. However, I feel the need to acknowledge my special debt to L. R. Scarborough and Raymond Calkins. I have to some extent used Scarborough's *How Jesus Won Men*[5] and Calkins' *How Jesus Dealt with Men*[6] as my models. Although both of those books are quite dated, they first shaped the dream of this volume in my mind.

Gaines S. Dobbins, along with Scarborough, was absolutely enamored with the idea of Jesus as the model evangelist. His *Evangelism According to Christ*[7] is one of the most seminal books in all of the nonbiblical literature on evangelism. Ideas from the last chapter of that volume are still hatching, growing, and matching in my mind. My guess is that through men like Scarborough and Dobbins, one of the important contributions of Southern Baptists to evangelism has been an intentional development of the idea that Jesus Christ is the evangelist without a peer.

Robert Coleman's *They Meet the Master*[8] is a short workbook approach to studying cases in the evangelism of Jesus. That little volume may be used by an individual or a group. I personally like it more than Coleman's much better known volume, *The Master Plan of Evangelism.*[9]

Another even briefer workbook which has helped me is Fred E. White's *Follow Me and I Will Make You Fishers of Men.* White says it is a devotional guidebook to help us develop an evangelistic life-style. Thirty cases are treated, one a day for a month.[10] Those who work seriously through this little devotional guide for Christian witnesses will be richly rewarded.

A friend recommended that I read David L. McKenna's *The Jesus Model* in preparation for my study of these cases. If you read it, pay close attention to chapter 11, "Jesus, Our Model."[11]

Two recent volumes which I have found rewarding are James E. Carter's *Christ and the Crowds* and Jerry Vines's *Interviews with Jesus.*[12] Carter treats how Jesus dealt with persons collectively and individually. Vines gives an exposition of eleven cases with which Jesus dealt.

Notes

1. See Delos Miles, *Master Principles of Evangelism* (Nashville: Broadman Press, 1982).
2. See Leighton Ford, *The Christian Persuader* (New York: Harper & Row, Publishers, 1966), p. 67.
3. See Herschel H. Hobbs, *New Testament Evangelism* (Nashville: Convention Press, 1960), p. 70.
4. The performance was based on the edition by H. Watkins Shaw.
5. L. R. Scarborough, *How Jesus Won Men* (Grand Rapids: Baker Book House, 1972 reprint).
6. Raymond Calkins, *How Jesus Dealt with Men* (New York: Abingdon-Cokesbury Press, 1942).
7. Gaines S. Dobbins, *Evangelism According to Christ* (Nashville: Broadman Press, 1949).
8. Robert E. Coleman, *They Meet the Master* (Huntingdon Valley, PA: Christian Outreach, 1973).
9. Robert E. Coleman, *The Master Plan of Evangelism* (Westwood, NJ: Fleming H. Revell Co., 1963).
10. Fred E. White, *Follow Me and I Will Make You Fishers of Men* (Lutherville, MD: Baptist Convention of Maryland Press, 1978 rev. ed.).
11. David L. McKenna, *The Jesus Model* (Waco, TX: Word Books, Publisher 1977), see especially pp. 169-79.
12. Both volumes are by Broadman Press, 1981.

1

A Woman in the House of Simon
Proverbs 17:17; Luke 7:31-50

Back in the 1960s a pastor invited me to speak to his leaders on evangelism. He suggested I might want to center my remarks around friendship evangelism. At that time I could find no complete books which treated the subject.

However, the situation is quite different now. A Mennonite pastor, Arthur G. McPhee published his book on *Friendship Evangelism* in 1978.[1] Then, in 1979 Wayne McDill, a Southern Baptist pastor, published *Making Friends for Christ*.[2] Both of these books are indebted to the research done by church growth movement leaders such as Donald McGavran and Win Arn. An increasing amount of literature is being produced, which relates to friendship evangelism.[3]

Nevertheless, I knew a long time before the 1960s that Jesus had pointed the way in friendship evangelism. I invite you to look with me now at a case which reveals that Jesus was a friend to sinners. This case is found in the Gospel of Luke. Luke, as you may know, has been called "the Gospel to the Outcasts." If we are ever going to see our Lord as *the* friend of sinners, we shall certainly see that in the Third Gospel.

Please consider seven observations in connection with the case of the woman in the house of Simon. Each of them begins with the letter "C." They center around the words: contrast, courtesies, contribution, cruse, concern, confrontation, and curiosity.

Contrast

Contrast is sometimes useful in evangelism. Jesus used it often. He contrasted the Pharisee and the publican; the two sons; the prodigal and the elder brother.

Note the contrast in this case between the two sinners: Simon and the woman. Simon was a Pharisee. He belonged to that same party as did Gamaliel and Saul of Tarsus. Clearly, he was among Israel's finest. The woman was a prostitute who sold her body for a living.

Simon was a male who had doubtlessly been circumcised on the eighth day. His badge of belonging to Israel was beyond denial. The prostitute was a woman who was a "sinner" and an outcast. She belonged to the weaker, less privileged sex of Israel.

Simon was well-to-do, powerful, proud, well educated, and possibly wealthy. The woman appears to have been one of the poor and powerless of the earth. Gone were her virtue and her reputation.

Simon was conscious of no need in his life. He was self-sufficient. The woman was so overwhelmed with her need that she even loosed her hair in public. For any Jewish woman to appear with unbound hair was a grave act of immodesty. Simon saw himself as a good man in the sight of men and God. The woman saw herself as the lowest of sinners. Isn't it strange that the better a person truly is, the more he or she feels his or her sin? Francis of Assisi said, "There is nowhere a more wretched and miserable sinner than I."

See also the contrast between the attitude of Jesus and Simon toward sinners. Simon said to himself, "If this man were a prophet, he would have known who and what sort of woman this is who is touching him, for she is a sinner" (v. 39). Simon's attitude was that Jesus should have nothing to do with such a woman.

If we look at the paragraph immediately preceding the actual case in verses 31-35, the contrast between the attitude of Simon and Jesus is highlighted. They said of Jesus, "Behold, a glutton and a drunkard, a friend of tax collectors and sinners!" (v. 34). Those who said that were at least half right. Jesus was "a friend of tax collectors and sinners." As they say in Virginia, "He was that!" By following that saying with the case of the woman in the house of Simon, Luke wants us to see that his major point is to illustrate that Jesus was, in fact, a friend to all sinners.

One of the very first things we have to settle in order to be effective witnesses to Jesus Christ is our attitude toward persons. If we don't believe persons are worth saving, we shall not so much as lift one little finger to save them.

Peter was right. Love does indeed cover a multitude of sins (1 Pet. 4:8). Are we a friend to sinners or a foe? Do we attract them, or do we drive them away? Still a third contrast to notice in this case is that between two concepts of mission. Simon, the Pharisee, seems to see his mission as that of making Pharisees out of persons. Jesus, on the other hand, sees his mission as that of forgiving sinners their sins.

If God were in the cloning business, and should choose to clone all persons from Simon the Pharisee, what kind of world would this be? Perish the thought! Our mission is not to "shut the kingdom of heaven against men," but to open the door and invite them to come in (see Matt. 23:13). Our mission is the same as that of Jesus, to seek and to save the lost.

Courtesies

Common courtesies, and the way we respond to them, are revealing in evangelism. Simon invited Jesus to eat with him. Jesus would not readily pass up a good meal. Although he was no glutton, he was surely no ascetic who always fasted instead of feasting.

More than that, a good place to witness is around the dinner table. You see, Jesus was not simply a friend to the woman. He was also a friend to Simon. Jesus was a friend to the "up and outs" as well as to the "down and outs."

Simon extended a courtesy to Jesus by inviting him to dine in his house. Jesus reciprocated by accepting the invitation. We can be sure that Jesus wanted to be Simon's friend as much as he wanted to be the prostitute's friend.

I am coming to feel that there are few better places to evangelize in all the world than around our own table or around someone else's. Somehow the barriers to communication break down rather quickly around a good meal.

How long has it been since you invited a lost person to dine with you? How long has it been since you accepted an invitation to eat with a lost person? Such a repast in your own home or in the home of another is even more appropriate for evangelism than in some public restaurant. Yet, the real courtesies in this case were extended by the acknowledged sinner. Hear what Jesus said to Simon: "I entered your house, you gave me no water for my feet, but she has wet my feet with her tears and wiped them with her hair. You gave me no kiss, but from the time I came in she has not ceased to kiss my feet. You did not anoint my head with oil, but she has anointed my feet with ointment" (vv. 44-46).

Simon was derelict in extending such common social courtesies to Jesus as offering water for washing his feet, and extending him a kiss of brotherhood. The woman more than made up for all those courtesies which Simon overlooked.

Cordiality does tell us something in our evangelism. The perceptive witness will take note of all courtesies extended toward him or her, as well as all those which are not offered. Moreover, the witness will, like his or her Lord, be quick to receive all courtesies in the spirit they are offered.

Contrition

Our third word for analyzing this case is contrition. Which person exhibited a broken and a contrite heart? This woman's tears and kisses were more eloquent than words. Did not King David say, "A broken and contrite heart, O God, thou wilt not despise" (Ps. 51:17)?

Jesus does not cast out any sinner who comes to him for forgiveness. As he himself said, "Him who comes to me I will not cast out" (John 6:37). The prophet Isaiah puts it this way, "A bruised reed he will not break, and a dimly burning wick he will not quench" (Isa. 42:3).

Therefore, let the weak and the broken come to Jesus. Let those whose fire is about to go out come to him. He will not snuff out those with but a little fire. He will fan the sparks into a flame!

Perhaps we should learn to look for contrition in the cases with which we deal. One of the most interesting facts about this case is that the prostitute never uttered a word from start to finish. Her actions spoke for her. Those of us who are in the habit of listening for the right words from our prospects may be better advised to listen for a person's broken heart. The only formula our Lord requires is genuine contrition for one's sins. While right words have their place, the marks of contrition point us more surely to repentance.

If our Lord does not refuse such a one, how dare we? Is the servant ever greater than his or her Lord?

Cruse

A fourth insight into this case may be gained by reflecting upon the cruse of ointment. It was an alabaster flask of ointment, the most precious treasure the woman owned. With that sweet-smelling stuff, she prepared her own body for the practice of her profession.

The cruse of alabaster which she broke is symbolic of her break with the past. By that costly act she signaled that her old life was over.

Please note that the woman anointed the feet of Jesus with the precious ointment. Simon did not even spare a little olive oil to anoint his head. She, however, gave the most precious possession she had to anoint his feet! What a contrast.

Mark you well, when a sinner comes to Jesus with such a cruse and offers it to him as a token of her love, the Savior will not refuse such love and generosity. He will take note of it.

Concern

Concern bleeds through in our evangelism even in the absence of dialogue. Jesus said far more to Simon than he did to the woman. According to the text, Jesus only made two statements to the woman: "Your sins are forgiven" (v. 48); and "Your faith has saved you; go in peace" (v. 50).

Nevertheless, Jesus did communicate his loving concern through his body language and through his words to Simon. If Jesus had refused to let the lady anoint his feet and wipe them with her hair, he might have rejected her by drawing back.

The fact that the woman focused on the feet of Jesus says a great deal to us. The head was the focal point of the body in her society. Yet, she wet his feet with her tears. She wept over his feet. Apparently his feet had not been washed. Still she continually kissed his dusty feet and wiped them with her long, loose hair. It was his feet which she anointed and not his head.

Perhaps her focus upon the feet instead of the head shows us how

lowly she felt in his presence. She may not have considered herself
worthy to anoint his head. Moreover, we cannot help but remember the
word of Isaiah which Paul quoted, "How beautiful are the feet of those
who preach good news!" (Rom. 10:15).

Incidentally, we should not suppose that the woman was an intruder
in the house of Simon. Probably the meal was held outdoors in the
courtyard. Many of the wealthy in the days of Jesus built their homes
around a courtyard. They ate out-of-doors in that courtyard when
weather permitted. It was customary when one entertained a famous
guest for passersby to come in and listen to the conversation. Therefore, having heard that this famous rabbi was dining with Simon, the
woman seized this opportunity to show her love for him.

Persons did not eat at tables like we do today. They ate reclining on
their left elbows with their feet extended behind them. That explains
how the woman could get to Jesus' feet from behind him as the text
states.

We actually communicate more at times through our body language
than we do through our words. There is, of course, a vital and essential
place for words in our witnessing. But the tone of those words and the
way we utter them with the various members of our body communicate
our concern for persons.

I am struck in this case not only by the absence of any words from the
woman, but also by the relative paucity of words by Jesus to the
woman. Whether we use few words or many in our witnessing, our
concern will bleed through to those with whom we deal.

The reverse is also true. Our lack of concern and love will also bleed
through, even though that unconcern may not be voiced. Jesus read
Simon like a book. When Simon was talking to himself, Jesus read his
thoughts (see vv. 39-40). Simon's countenance gave him away. Jesus
read his negative thoughts.

Confrontation

Everyone loves a story. Jesus confronted Simon with the story of two
debtors. "A certain creditor had two debtors; one owed five hundred
denarii, and the other fifty. When they could not pay, he forgave them
both. Now which of them will love him more?" (vv. 41-42). Five

hundred denarii would have been equal to about $100.00 in our money. Jesus forced Simon to articulate the obvious. Note that Simon said, "I suppose . . . " (v. 43). This was clearly a confrontation of Simon by Jesus. The question, "Now which of them will love him more?" was put directly to Simon. Jesus invited Simon's personal opinion in the confrontation.

There does come a time when we need to forthrightly confront persons in our witnessing. Jesus did. Robert Coleman summarizes the kind of confrontation we should make in these words, "Gentleness with the weak; severity with the strong—these are the marks of a sensitive evangelist."[4]

Curiosity

Curiosity about Jesus is not to be equated with conversion to Jesus. Simon was merely curious. There is no confession of sin on his part. He missed the significance of Jesus' coming.

The question stated by those at the table with Jesus, "Who is this, who even forgives sins?" (v. 49), reflects only curiosity. Interest in Jesus is not enough to save a person. The world has that. There must be sincere openness to truth and worship of God. Only those who put their trust in Jesus go away in peace.

Evidently Simon had invited Jesus to dine with him because he thought he was a prophet. That belief had been shattered, "If this man were a prophet, he would have known who and what sort of woman this is who is touching him" (v. 39). Now, this man, whom he mistakenly thought was a prophet, had the audacity to forgive sins!

There is an old saying that it was curiosity which killed the cat. I don't know about that, but I do know that mere curiosity is never to be equated with conversion. No matter how much persons may wonder who Jesus is, they will never know until they trust themselves to him and to his saving power.

The woman apparently saw something in Jesus beyond that of a prophet. Her humility before Jesus, as she wept over his feet and anointed them, may indicate that she saw herself as his slave and him as her Lord.

Notes

1. Arthur G. McPhee, *Friendship Evangelism: The Caring Way to Share Your Faith* (Grand Rapids: Zondervan Publishing House, 1978).

2. Wayne McDill, *Making Friends for Christ* (Nashville: Broadman Press, 1979).

3. See the following: Jim Petersen, *Evangelism as a Lifestyle* (Colorado Springs, CO: NavPress Publishing Co., 1980); George G. Hunter III, *The Contagious Congregation: Frontiers in Evangelism & Church Growth* (Nashville: Abingdon Press, 1979), esp. pp. 35-63; Richard Stoll Armstrong, *Service Evangelism* (Philadelphia: The Westminster Press, 1979); C. B. Hogue, *Love Leaves No Choice: Life-Style Evangelism* (Waco, TX: Word Books, Publisher, 1976); Ralph W. Neighbour, Jr. and Cal Thomas, *Target-Group Evangelism* (Nashville: Broadman Press, 1975); Michael Green, *Evangelism in the Early Church* (Grand Rapids: Wm. B. Eerdmans, Publishing Co., 1970), esp. pp. 207-23; and Ralph W. Neighbour, Jr., Compiler, *Future Church* (Nashville: Broadman Press, 1980), esp. the chapter by Tom Wolf on "Oikos Evangelism: Key to the Future," pp. 153-76.

What Arthur McPhee calls *friendship* evangelism, is called *relational* evangelism by Wayne McDill, *affirmation* evangelism by Petersen, *inductive* evangelism by Hunter, *service* evangelism by Armstrong, *life-style* evangelism by Hogue, *target-group* evangelism by Neighbour and Thomas, *household* evangelism by Green, and *oikos* evangelism by Wolf. I call it *web* evangelism in my *Church Growth—A Mighty River* (Nashville: Broadman Press, 1981), p. 127. I am indebted to Donald A. McGavran for the term.

4. Robert E. Coleman, *They Meet the Master* (Huntingdon Valley, PA: Christian Outreach, 1973), p. 61.

2

John's Disciples
Daniel 7:13-14; John 1:35-51

John the Baptist played a prominent role in the ministry of Jesus. He was the forerunner of Jesus, who claimed nothing more for himself than to be a voice in the wilderness crying out, "Make straight the way of the Lord" (John 1:23).

It was John who baptized Jesus in the Jordan River. It was John who tied ethics and social action to his evangelism when the multitudes asked him, "What then shall we do?" (Luke 3:10).

And he answered them, "He who has two coats, let him share with him who has none; and he who has food, let him do likewise." Tax collectors also came to be baptized, and said to him, "Teacher, what shall we do?" And he said to them, "Collect no more than is appointed you." Soldiers also asked him, "And we, what shall we do?" And he said to them, "Rob no one by violence or by false accusation, and be content with your wages" (Luke 3:11-14).

We can indeed learn much about evangelism from John the Baptist. Moreover, we can learn some things about evangelism from the disciples of John, and even more about it from Jesus himself. The case of John's disciples uniquely combines lessons about evangelism from all three of these sources.

How and Why Persons Find Christ

The case of John's disciples tells us how, and to some extent why, persons find Christ. Some persons find Christ because others who know him point them to him. John the Baptist, who knew Christ, said to two of his disciples as he looked at Jesus, "Behold, the Lamb of God!"

(v. 36). The Scripture says of those two disciples that they heard John "and they followed Jesus" (v. 37).

Some persons find Christ because they seek him as did the two disciples of John, and as did Nicodemus. Oliver Cromwell wrote to his daughter: "To be a seeker is to be of the best sect next to a finder." Jesus said, "Seek and you shall find."

Some find Christ because those who know him bring them to him. Such was the case with Peter who was brought to Christ by Andrew. Also, this was true of Nathanael who was brought to Christ by Philip.

Still others find Christ because they are found by Christ as was Philip. The Scripture says of Philip's conversion, "And he found Philip and said to him, 'Follow me!' " (v. 43). More persons than Francis Thompson have found that Jesus Christ is "The Hound of Heaven" who pursues them down all the labyrinthine ways of life.

Persons find Christ for a multitude of reasons and through various ways. But we can be sure that some find Christ because they are first found and brought to him by the friends of Christ. I am struck by the use of the word *found* in the case of John's disciples. Three times that word is used in the case, once of Jesus (in v. 43) and twice of the disciples of Jesus (vv. 41,45).

Some lost persons may never find Christ unless the friends of Christ find them and bring them to him. Our God is a seeking God. Jesus said of his mission, "For the Son of Man came to seek and to save the lost" (Luke 19:10). Please note that Christ did not come only to save the lost but also to seek them. If we would pattern our evangelism after that of Jesus, we have no choice but to seek the lost for our Savior.

The Chain Reaction in Evangelism

A second lesson which we may learn from the case of John's disciples is that chain reactions do occur in evangelism. John the Baptist points two of his disciples to Jesus. One of the two was Andrew. The unnamed one may have been John, the son of Zebedee and the brother of James.

Andrew found his brother, Simon Peter. As a matter of fact, wherever you see Andrew he is bringing someone to Christ. It was Andrew who brought the lad with the few loaves and fishes to Christ. It was Andrew who brought the Greeks to Christ. Somehow when they came to Philip, he thought it wise to bring them to Andrew who brought them to Jesus. Jesus found Philip, who was of Bethsaida, the hometown of Andrew and Peter. Philip found Nathanael, his friend, and invited him to come and see Jesus for himself.

That which began with John pointing two of his disciples to Jesus continued in a very brief span from the two of them to Simon Peter, Philip and Nathanael. Two became five. That is quick spiritual reproduction. While it may not be spiritual multiplication, it is the kind of spiritual addition and chain reaction in evangelism which can lead to the desired multiplication.

We might even point to Philip's part of this chain reaction as an example of spiritual multiplication. If we call what John did with his two disciples spiritual addition and if we include the witness of those two disciples with that of Jesus to Philip and call that spiritual reproduction, then Philip's witness to Nathanael could be properly called spiritual multiplication. Nathanael might well represent the fruit of spiritual reproduction. At least as the story is structured, we may consider him a fourth generation disciple via John the Baptist, the two disciples of John and Philip.

This kind of chain reaction is really what we are after in evangelism. It accounts for Dawson Trotman making 2 Timothy 2:2 the golden text of his life. Four generations of witnesses are mentioned in that text: Paul, Timothy, "faithful men," and "others." Timothy is Paul's son in the faith. He is to pass on what Paul had entrusted to him "to faithful men who will be able to teach others also." Hence, the living chain of witnesses ever lengthens itself by adding new links through spiritual reproduction and multiplication.

Dawson Trotman interpreted his golden text to mean that we Christians are born to reproduce. In other words, if there were just one Christian in the world and that Christian reproduced himself every six months, and everyone won did likewise, at the end of fifteen and one-half years there would be 2,176,000,000 Christians in the world![1]

That figure is astonishing. Nevertheless, it is accurate and possible. Theoretically, John R. Mott's famous slogan, "The World for Christ in This Generation," is possible even in a world with four billion inhabitants. But such a slogan will never become a reality unless many such chain reactions as we read about in John 1 take place.

The Role of Kinship and Friendship

A third lesson to be learned from the case of John's disciples is the role of kinship and friendship in evangelism. John the Baptist was both a friend to his two disciples and to Jesus. He had already established his credibility with Andrew and the other unnamed disciple. Therefore, when he pointed them to Jesus, they heard and readily responded. When a friend whom you believe and trust tells you something, you believe him. Therefore, friendship can play an important role in evangelism.

Philip was doubtlessly a friend of Andrew and Peter. He was from their hometown. My guess is that Jesus sought and found Philip because Andrew and Peter had told him what a fine disciple Philip would make.

When Philip got saved, he found his friend Nathanael and said, "We have found him of whom Moses in the law and also the prophets wrote, Jesus of Nazareth, the son of Joseph" (v. 45). The ensuing dialogue between Nathanael and Philip reveals that they were good friends. They could level with each other. Perhaps there is even a touch of humor in the question which Nathanael put to Philip, "Can anything good come out of Nazareth?" (v. 46).

Hence, we see how the gospel moved forward on the wings of friendship in the case of John's disciples. What an inexhaustible supply of prospective Christians is furnished by the network of friendships.

Robert Hastings, the editor of the *Illinois Baptist,* tells how many years ago he visited with the First Baptist Church of Fort Worth, Texas, one Wednesday night when Pastor J. Frank Norris was talking to his Sunday School teachers. Pastor Norris said:

> The best prospects for this church are the members and friends of those in this room. As you reach them, broaden your circle of friends. If you work this ever-enlarging circle of people, you'll never run out of prospects. You needn't waste your time knocking on doors of strangers.[2]

Pastor Norris was a self-appointed castigator of Southern Baptists, but he let his Sunday School teachers in on an important insight regarding the discovery of prospects. The friends of our church members are some of the best prospects we shall ever have. Moreover, our personal friends who are away from God are some of the best witnessing opportunities we shall ever have.

Somewhat the same things may be said with even greater certainty regarding our kinfolk. The first thing Andrew did after he had found Christ was to go and find his own brother and bring him to Jesus. I imagine I can almost hear Andrew saying with genuine excitement, "Simon, Simon, come quickly with me; we have found the Messiah" (see vv. 41-42).

It is possible for us to lead our kinfolk to Christ. Andrew did, and so can we. Whoever said we are too close to our own family members to lead them to Christ was dead wrong. On the contrary, the most likely person in all the world to lead your family to Christ is you, or some other member of your family.

Your deepest relationships are your best witnessing opportunities. Why should we expect some stranger to be more successful than we in winning to Christ our family and kinfolk? If our faith doesn't make an impact on those nearest and dearest to us, why should we expect strangers to believe us? Surely, if we have been changed by the power of God, some of the folk most likely to notice the difference our faith makes in our daily living will be the members of our nuclear and extended family.

That saying about charity beginning at home may be debatable, depending on what you mean by charity. But to say that evangelism begins at home is to speak the unadulterated truth. What better persons are there to win one's own children to Christ than their Christian parents? What better persons are there among us to win the lost Simon Peters than the Andrews?

Could it be that our refusal to try to win our own kinfolk to Christ is a cop-out? Does our abdication of that solemn responsibility to strangers and to outside experts say something about the poverty of our own Christian life-style?

Win Arn, of the Institute for American Church Growth, asked over 8,000 church members in many denominations, "Why are most of the people in your church part of your church?" The answers to this question revealed that friends or relatives accounted for 70 to 90 percent of all church members.[3]

We should learn from the case of John's disciples that both kinship and friendship are the bridges across which God usually moves into the lives of others. Each Christian has a natural web of kinship, friendship, and other relationships which God wants to use to trumpet the good news, "Behold, the Lamb of God, who takes away the sin of the world!" (John 1:29).

How to Deal with Doubt

A fourth lesson to be learned from this case is the wise way to deal with honest doubt in evangelism. Doubt is omnipresent in many witnessing encounters. Even when it is not expressed, we can be sure it is often present.

When Nathanael said, "Can anything good come out of Nazareth?" (v. 46), he was expressing his doubt. Did that make Philip uptight? Not in the least. Philip didn't start lecturing his friend on the pitfalls of doubt. Rather, quietly and simply he said, "Come and see" (v. 46).

"Come and see." That is the appropriate way to deal with doubt. Those are the identical words of Jesus to the two disciples of John (see John 1:39). When they put a question to him, he gave them an invitation to "Come and see." Accordingly, when Nathanael put a question to Philip, Philip followed the example of Jesus and said, "Come and see." Every question put to us in evangelism does not require a refutation. All some questions require is an invitation to "Come and see."

Do not demand certainty until you have made the experiment. "Taste and see that the Lord is good." The proof of the pudding is in the eating.

Honest doubt can become the cutting edge of faith. As Tennyson said, "There lies more faith in honest doubt, Believe me, than in half the creeds." We can be sure that all honest doubts will ultimately be shipwrecked on the solid rock of faith in the Lord Jesus Christ.

The Supernatural Element

A fifth lesson lifted up for us in the case of John's disciples is the supernatural element in evangelism. There is an undeniable supernatural element in all true evangelism. That is true because evangelism is spiritual work done by persons who have spiritual power. Strangely enough, in this case and in most cases recorded in the Gospel of John, that supernatural element is expressed most strongly in the special knowledge which Jesus has of Simon and Nathanael. When Jesus looked at Simon, he said, "So you are Simon the son of John? You shall be called Cephas" (v. 42). Now, Cephas means Peter, or rock. The Aramaic word for rock is *Cephas,* and the Greek word is *Peter.* Somehow, Jesus knew that this rough and rugged, cursing fisherman was more like a rock than anything else. So, he changed his name to something like our "Rocky." Whatever Simon may have been at the time he first met Jesus, he later became a kind of Rock of Gibraltar in the apostolic church.

Note the surprise of Nathanael. Before Nathanael had ever spoken to Jesus, Jesus said of him, "Behold, an Israelite indeed, in whom is no guile!" (v. 47). Nathanael said, "How do you know me?" (v. 48). The answer of Jesus reveals that "he knew what was in man" (John 2:25): "Before Philip called you, when you were under the fig tree, I saw you" (v. 48).

However you square this special knowledge which Jesus had of persons such as Nathanael and Peter with Paul's words in Philippians about the self-emptying of Jesus (see Phil. 2:7), you will not wish to ignore such a prominent feature of our Lord's evangelism in the Gospel of John. That supernatural element for us may be expressed in terms of the plus and power which the Holy Spirit adds to our witnessing. It might even be seen in the element of divine forgiveness which occurs in evangelism. The point to remember is that there is a transcendent dimension in our evangelism which we dare not overlook.

The Kingdom in Evangelism

The last lesson which I lift up from the case of John's disciples has to do with the role of the kingdom of God in evangelism. Nathanael confessed, "Rabbi, you are the Son of God! You are the King of Israel!" (v. 49).

Jesus accepted that confession, but took Nathanael a long step beyond it, "Truly, truly, I say to you, you will see heaven opened, and the angels of God ascending and descending upon the Son of man" (v. 51). That is a reference to the passage in Daniel 7:13-14.

> I saw in the night visions,
> and behold, with the clouds of heaven
> there came one like a son of man,
> and he came to the Ancient of Days
> and was presented before him.
> And to him was given dominion
> and glory and kingdom,
> that all peoples, nations and languages
> should serve him;
> his dominion is an everlasting dominion,
> which shall not pass away,
> and his kingdom one
> that shall not be destroyed.

In other words, Jesus claimed to be the fulfillment of Daniel's prophecy. Jesus claimed that he himself was the ladder to heaven. Moreover, his dominion is over all and everlasting. He is the King of that kingdom which has come, and is yet to come.

Hence, we see both inclusiveness and exclusiveness in the kingdom of God. Included in the kingdom are "all people, nations, and languages." Yet, the King of that kingdom defines its character. He determines how his kingdom will be entered.

Those who would enter his kingdom except through him are thieves and robbers. "I am the way, and the truth, and the life; no one comes to the Father, but by me" (John 14:6) says Jesus. The words of Acts 4:12 put the same point more plainly, "And there is salvation in no one else, for there is no other name under heaven given among men by which we must be saved."

If that exclusiveness offends anyone, so be it. We are not at liberty to remove it. There is indeed a narrowness about the way which leads to eternal life.

Perhaps a final word about the kingdom of God in John's Gospel would help us here. John doesn't say much about the kingdom as such. There are, of course, a few references to the kingdom in John 3. However, mostly John uses euphemisms for the kingdom such as "eternal life." Therefore, it is rather striking to see this clear reference to the kingdom in the case of John's disciples.

Notes

1. Quoted by Waylon B. Moore, *New Testament Follow-Up* (Grand Rapids: Wm. B. Eerdmans Publishing Co., 1970, rev. ed.), p. 63.
2. Quoted by Robert S. Hastings in "The Best-Kept Secret About Church Growth: Start in Your Own Backyard," *Illinois Baptist,* February 7, 1979, p. 4.
3. Win Arn, "People Are Asking, . . . " *Church Growth: America,* Vol. 5, No. 2, p. 11.

3

Legion

Psalm 77:11-20; Mark 5:1-20

Look with me at the case of Legion. You may prefer to call this the case of the Gerasene demoniac. It is recorded for us in Mark 5:1-20. Parallels to the case may be found in Luke 8:26-39 and in Matthew 8:28-34.

No Case Too Hard

The first point which deeply impresses me about the case of Legion is that no case is too hard for Jesus, the strong Son of God. "What god is great like our God? Thou art the God who workest wonders" (Ps. 77:13b-14a).

"What is your name?" Jesus said to the Gerasene demoniac. "My name is Legion; for we are many" (v. 9), he said. This poor soul was so confused about his identity that he thought of himself as a legion of demons. Luke, in fact, adds this statement after Legion's name, "for many demons had entered him" (8:30). A Roman legion would have been about five to six thousand men.

However you choose to define demons and to explain that text, you will have to admit that something terrible had happened to this man. Legion was in a bad fix. He was a man possessed by negative, destructive, and antilife forces.

This person was driven by alien powers. He had been driven away from his family, friends, and community. He was in fact driven away from society itself. All normal contacts and social intercourse with other human beings had been cut off. He was engulfed in tragic loneliness.

These alien beings who had captured him must have driven him almost insane.

From my earliest recollections, I was told that if I didn't behave myself and be a good boy, the "bogeyman" would get me. The bogeyman was the devil, I was told, so I grew up believing in the devil and all sorts of bogies such as ghosts and evil trolls. One day, while alone in the woods, I thought I actually saw the devil. You know what he looked like? That picture of the red devil with horns on his head and a pitchfork in his hands on the Red Devil lye cans which we bought.

Nowadays such images are conjured up with games. For example, "Dungeons and Dragons" is a parlor game which became popular in 1981. Manufactured by TSR, Incorporated of Lake Geneva, Wisconsin, the game invites players to create a fantasy world of characters and deities. One evangelist and businessman in Kansas sought to have the game removed from stores on the grounds that it conjured up demons, witches, spells, and sorcery which he called "a wolf in lamb's clothing."[1]

There were several times in my childhood when I thought the bogeyman was surely going to get me. Well, I can tell you the bogeyman had gotten Legion. He was in the grips of an evil force so powerful that it had almost destroyed him.

Four facts about Legion stand out. First, he made his home in the graveyard. The text says, "There met him out of the tombs a man with an unclean spirit, who lived among the tombs" (vv. 2-3). Luke is even plainer saying, "He lived not in a house but among the tombs" (Luke 8:27).

He was the living among the dead. He was so wild and antisocial that he could not live among the living. The tombs were his dwelling place. Although he was alive physically, he was dead spiritually. Legion needed to be raised from the death of sin and demonic possession.

Second, Legion was so strong that he could not be bound. Note the text, "And no one could bind him any more, even with a chain; for he had often been bound with fetters and chains, but the chains he wrenched apart, and the fetters he broke in pieces; and no one had the strength to subdue him" (vv. 3-4). Evidently, the forces which controlled him gave him a superhuman strength.

Third, Legion made frightening sounds and bruised himself with stones. "Night and day among the tombs and on the mountains he was always crying out, and bruising himself with stones" (v. 5). Matthew's account uses the phrase "so fierce that no one could pass that way" (Matt. 8:28) to indicate the fear which those cries brought to persons. Apparently, Legion not only had the reputation for scaring others, but he also hurt himself with stones.

A fourth fact which we know about Legion is that he wore no clothes. Mark implies this by the word *clothed* in verse 15. However, Luke is explicit, saying, "For a long time he had worn no clothes" (Luke 8:27). There was apparently no sense of shame about his nakedness.

Did you happen to catch the story about the twenty-six-year-old man who died in New York City in 1981, after being robbed of his clothes? He was just passing through on his way to Washington, DC. He was mugged once and stripped of most of his clothes. Hours later he was mugged again and stripped of his pants. A mob chased him naked through Times Square. They jeered and laughed at him. Some threw bottles at him. He ran past the hookers and junkies on Eighth Avenue, across Forty-Second Street, and into a subway seeking safety. Two police officers grabbed him, but with the mob behind him, he bolted. He jumped onto the subway tracks, and was either electrocuted or died of a heart attack, as the mob that chased him laughed.

He was said to be a normal, well-behaved young man, who didn't smoke or drink. In fact, when he left home for a job interview in Washington, he was wearing a tie and coat.[2] I believe he was frightened to death, scared out of his mind, and shamed to death to be in public with no clothes on his body.

The fact that Legion wore no clothes reveals just how far gone he was. When Adam and Eve ate the forbidden fruit, "Then the eyes of both were opened, and they knew that they were naked; and they sewed fig leaves together and made themselves aprons" (Gen. 3:7).

A human being covering his or her nakedness has become an almost universal symbol of civilization. In the case of Adam and Eve, the covering of their nakedness was a symbol that their eyes had now been opened to good and evil. Evidently, Legion was so out of touch with reality, and with civilization, that he was even unaware of his nakedness.

Surely if ever there was a hard case, Legion was it. He pictures the possibility before each of us. Life seems to be running out of control for some of us. "We are filled with fear or guilt or lust or greed or sorrow or despair. We are 'possessed' by a destructive habit. We may be beating or abusing ourselves, like Legion did with the stones."[3]

No case is too hard for Jesus. No one is so much a slave to Satan that Jesus Christ cannot make him or her a slave to God. No one is so deep in the darkness of sin and evil that Christ cannot make him or her a child of the light. Jesus is the world's greatest liberator. He can set us free from all of our bondages. As he himself said, "If the Son makes you free, you will be free indeed" (John 8:36). Hallelujah! What a Savior!

The Absence of Fear

Legion did not intimidate Jesus. Jesus was not afraid of him. Nor was he afraid of any person.

Like our Lord, we do not need to fear any person in the world, "For he who is in you is greater than he who is in the world" (1 John 4:4). God has not given us "a spirit of timidity but a spirit of power and love and self-control" (2 Tim. 1:7).

Sometimes the best thing we can do with the Legions whom we encounter is to call their bluff. Paul wrote to the Philippians, "Stand firm in one spirit, with one mind striving side by side for the faith of the gospel, and *not frightened in anything by your opponents.* This is a clear omen to them of their destruction, but of your salvation, and that from God" (Phil. 1:27-28, author's italics).

The three figures of speech which Paul used in those two verses are taken from the life of a soldier, an athlete, and an equestrian. As the soldier stands firm in battle and refuses to retreat, so we are to "stand firm in one spirit." As an athletic team strains every muscle to cooperate and thus win the prize, so we are to strive with one mind "side by side for the faith of the gospel." As the equestrian steadfastly refuses to be startled like his horse, so we are not to be "frightened in anything" by our opponents.

One of my former students told me how he was called to the home of a madman one night. The man was threatening to kill his wife and children. When he arrived, the madman waved his pistol and told him he would kill him, too. Patiently, firmly, and courageously, this pastor rescued the wife and children and in time led the man to Christ. I do not advocate that we Christians act foolishly in the midst of real and grave physical danger. But I do believe that we need not fear those who can kill the body (see Matt. 10:28).

The Power Encounter

The case of Legion teaches us that no case is too hard and that we need not be timid and fearful of persons in our evangelism. Also, this case reveals one of the clearest examples of what missiologists call the power encounter in evangelism. For example, a Consultation on World Evangelization was held in Pattaya, Thailand, in 1980. That Consultation issued "The Thailand Statement" which says in part:

We know that we are engaged in a spiritual battle with demonic forces. Evangelism often involves a power encounter, and in conversion Jesus Christ demonstrates that he is stronger than the strongest principalities and powers of evil by liberating their victims.[4]

That power encounter on foreign mission fields has sometimes taken the form of converts from animism and other religions burning their fetishes and smashing their idols in a public ceremony. Here in the case of Legion it takes the form of exorcism of the demons. Mark 5:6-13 records in precise details how the power of "Jesus, Son of the Most High God" encountered and drove out the demonic powers. The essence of this encounter may be caught up in the command of Jesus, "Come out of the man, you unclean spirit!" (v. 8).

The power encounter is no longer, if indeed it ever was, limited to foreign mission fields. The whole world is a mission field. Persons are in bondage to evil and demoniclike powers everywhere. We even have Satan worshipers in America. Many are into astrology and the occult. We should accordingly not be surprised to see a power encounter taking place in many conversions today.

Is there anything inappropriate about converted alcoholics pouring out their booze and smashing their bottles? Are converted drug addicts acting irrationally when they break and smash and burn the drugs and paraphernalia which have enslaved them? Can we not see in many cases a royal battle going on in the faces and body language of the children of darkness when they are being convicted by the power of the Holy Spirit? There is a sense in which some kind of power encounter takes place in every conversion. Satan does not give up his victims readily. He fights to hold his turf. Those of us who want to be effective in our evangelizing will give some attention to the power encounter. Let us not be so naive as to think that the powers of darkness are benign.

The Name in Evangelism

The case of Legion may also teach something about the use of the name in evangelism. Jesus asked the Gerasene demoniac, "What is your name?" (v. 9). Jesus knew that a person's name often reveals who he is in his character, and not merely what he is called. Legion's name revealed that he was confused about his identity. He was many and not one. It is as though Legion were saying: "I don't know who I am; I am a multitude, an army; I am not an individual person."

However, by asking his name, Jesus was seeking also to affirm his personhood. No human being ever gets so enslaved to the powers of evil that he or she ceases to have a name. Legion may not have known who he was, but he was somebody. He was a person precious to Jesus. The demons had stolen his identity and his name. Jesus came to restore his identity and to give him a new name.

What's in a name? One's identity, legal status, and often who one has been, and who his or her parents or peers or teachers hope he or she will become. So, let us learn in our witnessing to take seriously all the names of persons, including their nicknames.

There is another aspect to the use of the name in evangelism which the case of Legion lifts up for us. Note how Legion identifies the name of Jesus as "Jesus, Son of the Most High God" (v. 7). How did he know that name? Did the demons who possessed him have some special knowledge of that name? Or, were Mark, Luke, and Matthew trying to tell us something about naming the name of Jesus?

I do not believe there is any magic even in the name of Jesus. But I do believe there is power in that name. The angel of the Lord said to Mary, "You shall call his name Jesus, for he will save his people from their sins" (Matt. 1:21). Jesus is a new Joshua who leads his people out of the bondage of sin into the Promised Land. His name represents his character. It reveals his identity. Only as persons come to know who Jesus is can they discover who they are. We discover our identity in his identity. Hence, in all true evangelism we must at some point name the name of Jesus. His is the name above every other name. The name of Jesus is, therefore, the most precious name in all the world.

Persons *Versus* Profits

An unusual feature about the case of Legion is the drowning of the large herd of hogs and the way the citizens of that area "began to beg Jesus to depart from their neighborhood" (v. 17). As a matter of fact, my attention was first called to this case back in the 1950s by a radio preacher who took as his subject, "Hog Killing and No Hot Water." Having been reared on a farm, I knew how much very hot water we had to have at hog-killing time. So, that preacher instantly secured my attention when he announced his topic.

What happened? Although this was Jewish territory, "a great herd of swine was feeding there on the hillside" (v. 11). Jews aren't supposed to eat pork. Was this a bootlegging operation in pork?[5] Possibly so. Religious prohibitions notwithstanding, many persons love hog meat. I dearly love it myself. Therefore, if pork can't be obtained legally, it will be gotten illegally.

That may explain the strong, negative feelings expressed against Jesus by the citizens of "the country of the Gerasenes" (v. 1). No wonder they begged him to depart. He had inadvertently discovered a massive bootlegging operation in pork. Moreover, they seemed to blame Jesus for the destruction of their hogs.

My guess is that in this out-of-the-way place, guarded as it was by the Gerasene demoniac, their bootlegging business was quite safe. But when the demoniac was healed, that blew their cover.

Do you think the owners of those hogs cared about Legion? No. They cared more for their profits and their property. Legion was even useful to them so long as he scared people away from that territory where they raised their pork.

Jesus, on the contrary, always values persons above property and economic profits. He disturbs our illegal shenanigans. He upsets our greedy and shady dealings. He challenges our warped values and our corrupt morals. Besides, Jesus didn't kill those hogs. The demons did. Jesus doesn't go around destroying property, not even hogs. Remember, it was Jesus who said, "Not what goes into the mouth defiles a man, but what comes out of the mouth" (Matt. 15:11). It was those unclean spirits who entered the swine and caused them to commit suicide, not Jesus (see vv. 10-13).

Some persons will not welcome Jesus because he challenges their way of life. He sets an infinite value upon every human being. Persons are more important to Jesus than are profits and property and things. Alas! The Legions of our world are more valuable to some in their demon possessed state than they are "sitting, . . . clothed and in [their] right mind" (see v. 15).

At-Home Evangelism

The case of Legion also shows us that Jesus believes in at-home evangelism. While the citizens of the country begged Jesus to depart, the saved demoniac "begged him that he might be with him" (v. 18).

What a contrast! There are three kinds of beggars in this case. The demons begged to enter the swine. The people begged him to leave their neighborhood. The new man begged to go with him.

This demoniac might have been a "big-name" convert, traveling with Jesus and giving his testimony all over Palestine. He could have been "Exhibit A" of the power of Jesus to drive out a whole legion of demons. Surely, Legion might have helped draw large crowds to hear Jesus preach and teach. If ever a famous convert showed potential for becoming a star, it was Legion.

But hear the answer of Jesus to Legion's request, "Go home to your friends, and tell them how much the Lord has done for you, and how he has had mercy on you" (v. 19). Jesus actually refused to let Legion become a part of his entourage.

Our Lord believed in at-home evangelism. Evangelism begins at home. Let us not suppose that we shall be more successful at evangelizing strangers than we are at evangelizing our own families and relatives and friends. *The grass in evangelism is never greener abroad than it is in our own household.* How shall we do cross-cultural evangelism if we refuse to evangelize our own sphere of influence? The evangelism road which takes us to the uttermost parts of the earth begins at our own Jerusalem and Judea (see Acts 1:8).

There is a sequel to this story. Like a good Western movie, it has a happy ending. "And he went away and began to proclaim in the Decapolis how much Jesus had done for him; and all men marveled" (v. 20). Legion had more credibility with those at home who knew him than he had abroad with those who knew him not.

Main Qualification for a Witness

I cannot leave the case of Legion without observing that the main qualification for a Christian witness is that the Lord has done something for him or her. Legion had never taken my 156 Basic Evangelism course. Nor did he have courses 158 or 159 which I have taught. He didn't have any exposure to WIN (Witness Involvement Now), or to EE (Evangelism Explosion), or to any other formal training in witnessing.

The one thing Legion did have which qualified him to be a witness was that God had done some things for him. God had changed his life. He had been naked, but Jesus had clothed him with the righteousness of God. He had been possessed by demons; now he was possessed by the Holy Spirit. He had been out of his mind; now he was in his right mind. He had been bruising and hurting himself; now he was calm and at peace with himself, God, and others. He had been in "harm's way"; now he was in the heavenly way. Once he was lost; now he had been found. Once he had been blinded by the darkness of sin; now he saw clearly by the light of Christ.

If God has done anything great for you, then you have the primary qualification for being a witness.

Notes

1. See Karen Uhlenhuth, "Evangelist Exhorts Retailers to Drop 'Dungeons' Game," *The Kansas City Times,* June 17, 1981, B-9. See also Phyllis Ten

Elshof, "D & D: A Fantasy Fad or Dabbling in the Demoniac," *Christianity Today,* Vol. XXV, No. 15, Sept. 4, 1981, p. 56. This article reported that "Dungeons and Dragons" (D & D) had become the favorite past time of more than three million children and adults. One physician who played the game wrote in *Psychology Today* about the high level of violence in this make-believe world of D & D. "There is hardly a game," said the doctor, "in which the players do not indulge in murder, arson, torture, rape, or highway robbery."

2. See "Jeering Mob Brutally Cut Off Man's Hopes of 'Something Better,' " *The Kansas City Times,* July 2, 1981, p. A-5.

3. Joe Harding, "Stop Hurting Yourself and Start Living," *Church Growth: America,* Vol. 7, No. 1, p. 13.

4. See "The Thailand Statement" in *World Evangelization,* Information Bulletin No. 20, September, 1980, p. 7, a publication of the Lausanne Committee for World Evangelization.

5. I am indebted to Clarence Jordan for this suggestion. See Clarence Jordan's *The Substance of Faith and Other Cotton Patch Sermons,* Dallas Lee, ed. (New York: Association Press, 1972), pp. 36-37.

4

Nicodemus

Numbers 21:4-9; John 3:1-21

The case of Nicodemus is found only in John's Gospel, chapter 3:1-21. However, Numbers 21:4-9 is the Old Testament background to the case. Also, John 3:31-36 is a kind of commentary and continuation of the case. Furthermore, the Fourth Gospel mentions Nicodemus a second time in 7:50 and 19:39.

A Representative Man

While Nicodemus was a real flesh-and blood-person, he was at the same time a representative person. First, Nicodemus represented the knowledge which Jesus has of persons. The preceding chapter tells us that Jesus "knew all men and needed no one to bear witness of man; for he himself knew what was in man" (John 2:25). Immediately following that declaration, we are told about Nicodemus as an example of that knowledge which Jesus had of men.

Nicodemus is exhibit A of John 2:25. The woman at the well in John 4 is exhibit B. The way Jesus dealt with Nathanael in John 1 had pointed toward the statement in John 2:25.

Jesus knew a great deal about Nicodemus. We need to seek to know as much as possible about those to whom we bear witness. In fact, we ought to study our prospects as seriously as we study our Bibles. The more we know about our prospects, the better are our chances of leading them to Christ. It surely helps to know the name, address, occupation, telephone number, and character of potential disciples.

We cannot write off the knowledge which Jesus had of people *simply* by attributing it to his divinity. He was the divine Son of God. But this very Gospel tells us he was the Word made flesh, also. In fact, the apostle Paul tells us in Philippians 2:6-7 that "though he was in the form of God, [he] did not count equality with God a thing to be grasped, but emptied himself, taking the form of a servant."

Second, Nicodemus was a representative man in the sense that he was an example of the rabbis who came to Jesus and were saved. Saul of Tarsus, who became Paul the apostle to the Gentiles, was of course a rabbi whose life was revolutionized by Jesus Christ on the Damascus Road. But Nicodemus preceded Saul.

I would connect the conversion of Nicodemus, an official of Judaism, with that of the Jewish priests in Acts 6:7. Following the election of the seven we are told, "A great many of the priests were obedient to the faith." Josephus, the Jewish historian, tells us that there were about 20,000 priests at that time. Nicodemus may be considered the first fruit of a great harvest of converts from the officials of Judaism.

Third, Nicodemus may also be thought of as a representative man in the sense that he was a representative of the intellectuals, the wealthy, and highborn persons who have come to Jesus for salvation. Nicodemus was "a teacher of Israel" and "a ruler of the Jews." He invested a lot of money to give Jesus a decent burial. Even the intellectuals and wealthy and highborn need to be born again. And Nicodemus is a representative that all such persons can be saved.

Fourth, Nicodemus may be considered a representative of those would-be covert disciples who find that they must eventually go public with their faith in Jesus. The fact that he came to Jesus by night is mentioned each of the three times that the Fourth Gospel refers to him (see 3:2; 7:50; and 19:39, King James Version).[1]

Perhaps Nicodemus had hoped at first to keep his Christian discipleship secret. But see the progressive way in which the Gospel of John records how he had to go public with his faith. The incident recorded in John 7:40-52 brought Nicodemus to his feet saying, "Does our law judge a man without first giving him a hearing and learning what he does?" (7:51). That brought down on him the accusing question, "Are you from Galilee too?" (7:52).

Then, finally, after Jesus had been crucified, we are told that

Nicodemus "came bringing a mixture of myrrh and aloes, about a hundred pounds' weight" (John 19:39). In other words, he assisted Joseph of Arimathea, another secret disciple of Jesus, in lovingly and publicly giving Jesus a decent burial (see 19:38-42). It appears that as the risk became greater Nicodemus became bolder.

Fifth, Nicodemus was a representative man in the sense that what Jesus said to Nicodemus he says to us all. Note that Jesus said to Nicodemus, "Unless one is born anew, he cannot see the kingdom of God" (v. 3). That phrase "unless one" means unless any one and every one, Nicodemus and every one else besides.

What was necessary for Nicodemus is also necessary for you and me. We all have to be born again in order to see the kingdom of God. Jesus speaks a universal word to this representative of humanity. That's the reason Paul could make so much of the new creation.

One of the lessons about evangelism which we may learn from the case of Nicodemus is that he was a representative man as well as a real man. Is not that the case with every person to whom we bear witness? Is not every Homo sapiens a representative of the human species? Is not every lost person, at least in some respects, a representative of other lost persons? To know the one, is to begin to know the many. Hence, let us study each case, and more especially each outstanding case, so that we, too, might learn what is in man (see John 2:25).

Dialogue in Evangelism

I challenge you to study the case of Nicodemus to see the proper use of dialogue in evangelism. Even if we take the conversation between Jesus and Nicodemus to be a kind of verbatim by the fourth evangelist, allowing for possible omissions by the reporters, we can still see that Jesus was not practicing dump-truck evangelism on Nicodemus. Jesus had a dialogue with Nicodemus, not merely a monologue.

There was listening in that dialogue, on the part of both Jesus and Nicodemus. Listening to others is important in introducing them to the Savior.

Someone told me more than twenty-five years ago that I had to do all of the talking when I did evangelistic visitation. I was even told that I should always command and control the conversation. I have long since learned that I have to do as much or more listening than I do talking. Moreover, I have learned to listen to the Holy Spirit. If anyone controls the conversation, let it be the Holy Spirit. Note that the dialogue moved and progressed to an increasingly deeper level. The first section of the dialogue is in verses 2-3. The second part is in verses 4-8, and the final round in verses 9-21. G. Campbell Morgan says that in the first part of the dialogue Jesus and Nicodemus were talking face-to-face; in the second part they were conversing mind to mind; then, in the last part of the conversation they were speaking heart to heart.[2]

That might not be a bad pattern for us to follow in our witnessing. First, let us talk face-to-face. The face will usually communicate more than the voice. Second, let us talk with persons, mind to mind. We need not deny their intellect or ours. Third, let us seek to converse with potential converts heart to heart. Let us speak from the depth of our heart to the depth of their heart. After all, as Pascal observed, the heart has reasons of its own which logic and reason may not be able to compute.

A closer look at the dialogue will also reveal that it centered around questions and answers. The pivotal questions are from Nicodemus; but Jesus puts some questions of his own.

I once heard a person say: "Evangelism is listening to someone until he tells you his UC (Ultimate Concern), then you tell him about your J.C. (Jesus Christ)." That does seem to fit what Peter says in 1 Peter 3:15, "Always be prepared to make a defense to any one who calls you to account for the hope that is in you, yet do it with gentleness and reverence."

Three times in the dialogue Nicodemus raised a question, and Jesus answered it. The first question by Nicodemus is not stated. Nevertheless, it is implied, for the Scripture says, "Jesus answered him" (v. 3). Evidently the first question of Nicodemus had to do with entrance into the kingdom of God. His second question was really a twin question in verse 4. His third question was, "How can this be?" (v. 9).

Notice that Jesus gave specific answers to specific questions. Also, see that Jesus raised some questions of his own in 3:10-12. "Are you a teacher of Israel, and yet you do not understand this?" (v. 10). "If I have told you earthly things and you do not believe, how can you believe if I tell you heavenly things?" (v. 12).

Jesus was a master at asking questions. Sometimes the best way to answer a question is with a question, or with more than one question. I am committed to Socratic evangelism. Socrates was a master at asking questions which generated substantive answers. So was Jesus; and so should we endeavor to become, if we would pattern our witnessing after his.

For example, five of the questions which I have used in my witnessing are: (1) "Have you come to that point in your life where God has become more than just a word to you?" (2) "In your opinion, who is Jesus Christ?" (3) "In your opinion, what does one have to do in order to become a Christian?" (4) "Have you reached that place in your life where you know for certain that you will go to heaven when you die?" and, (5) "If you were to die right now, and stand before God in the judgment, and he were to say to you, 'Why should I let you into heaven?' what would you say?"

Dualism in Evangelism

We have seen thus far in the case of Nicodemus that he was a representative person, and that Jesus entered into a dialogue with him. A third point which the case lifts up for us is the use of dualism in witnessing. This case is chock-full of dualisms.

Two births are referred to in the case, a physical birth and a spiritual birth, the first birth and a second birth. Jesus said to Nicodemus, as he says to us all, "Unless one is born anew, he cannot see the kingdom of God" (v. 3). Nicodemus asked, "How can a man be born when he is old? Can he enter a second time into his mother's womb and be born?" (v. 4).

This is where we get our phrases "the new birth," "the second birth," "twice-born," "regeneration," and "born again." William James's classic study on "the twice-born type" and "the once-born type" religious experiences may be best understood in the light of the case of Nicodemus.[3]

All of the hullabaloo over being born again, which the press generated in connection with former President Jimmy Carter, has its biblical roots in the case of Nicodemus. Paul's emphasis on the "new creation" and the "new man" may ultimately trace back to the case of Nicodemus (see 2 Cor. 5:17). After all is said and done, what is an Adam II person but a twice-born person? And what is an Adam I person but a once-born person? (See Rom. 5:18-21; 1 Cor. 15:21-22.) What a magnificent piece of dualism does the case of Nicodemus generate around the two births!

Flesh and Spirit are a second dualism which the case lifts up. "That which is born of the flesh is flesh, and that which is born of the Spirit is spirit?" (v. 6). This duality fits the two births. The physical birth is flesh begetting flesh. The flesh can never beget anything but flesh. Everything after its own kind is a law of nature.

The spiritual birth is that which is born of the Spirit. Hence, the new birth is the work of the Holy Spirit, after the analogy of the virgin birth of our Lord. Just as that which was conceived in the womb of the virgin Mary was the work of the Holy Spirit, so when one is conceived and born into the family of God through the new birth, that is the work of the Holy Spirit.

Flesh and Spirit battle with each other in evangelism. They are the two main foes in that civil war which rages inside the individual. Hear what the apostle Paul said about it:

So I find it to be a law that when I want to do right, evil lies close at hand. For I delight in the law of God, in my inmost self, but I see in my members another law at war with the law of my mind and making me captive to the law of sin which dwells in my members. Wretched man that I am! Who will deliver me from this body of death? Thanks be to God through Jesus Christ our Lord! So then, I of myself serve the law of God with my mind, but with my flesh I serve the law of sin (Rom. 7:21-25).

A third dualism introduced in the case is that of earthly things *versus* heavenly things. "If I have told you earthly things and you do not believe, how can you believe if I tell you heavenly things?" (v. 12). Again, earthly things belong to the realm of flesh, the realm of the first birth which is physical; whereas heavenly things belong to the realm of the Spirit, or the new and second birth which is spiritual.

This earthly and heavenly dualism is taken farther in John 3:31-34. There the heavenly testimony is attested by the fact that God gives his

Spirit to his Son "not by measure" (v. 34). Implicitly in that commentary on the case is a dualism of witnesses and testimonies; one of which is an earthly witness and testimony, and the other a heavenly. We may conclude from all of this that the true witness to Jesus Christ and to the new birth is one who has been born of heaven, and whose testimony is given in the power of the Holy Spirit. He bears witness to what he has seen and heard (see v. 32).

Then, following close upon the earthly and heavenly dualism, we are introduced to the ascended and descended one. "No one has ascended into heaven but he who descended from heaven, the Son of man" (v. 13). Paul has a passage in Ephesians 4:8-10 which also uses this dualism of ascent and descent. Most likely the descent refers to the incarnation of Christ and the ascent to his resurrection and exhaltation over all others.

Both John and Paul may be using this duality to counteract incipient gnosticism, an early heresy which, among other things, taught that matter was evil and thus denied the reality of the incarnation of Jesus Christ. Hence, John may be saying something like this: "The new birth is possible only to those who trust themselves to the incarnate Christ who was crucified on the cross, raised from the grave, and exhalted above all other powers and principalities."

Other significant dualisms which may be observed in the case of Nicodemus are darkness and light, word and deed, love and wrath (or condemnation), perish and eternal life. Each of these is widely utilized in evangelism. Probably no more useful metaphors may be found in the Bible for building a theology of evangelism than those of light and darkness. Gabriel Fackre, a United Church of Christ theologian, has demonstrated how these biblical metaphors may be used to theologize on evangelism.[4]

First Peter 2:9 puts the purpose of the people of God in these words: "That you may declare the wonderful deeds of him who called you out of darkness into his marvelous light." Paul's call to the Gentiles is, "To open their eyes, that they may turn from darkness to light and from the power of Satan to God" (Acts 26:18). There is a biblical sense in which what we call evangelism is changing the children of darkness into the citizens of the kingdom of light.

The word and deed duality is quite useful to us in evangelization. In John's Gospel there is never a word without a deed, and never a deed without a corresponding word. Word and deed are perfectly conjoined in the Fourth Gospel. Indeed, "The Word became flesh" (1:14). Word and deed are joined in the great verse, John 3:16. The word is, "For God so loved the world." The deed is, "That he gave his only begotten Son" (KJV). God never loves us with mere words. He loves us with deeds which meet our needs. That is the nature of *agape* love.

Let not man put asunder what God has joined together. We need both words and deeds in our evangelism today. Our deeds of love and mercy and justice authenticate our words of truth. If our evangelism is to have credibility, we must combine our deeds with our words.

Have you ever noticed the dualism of love and wrath in John 3? The same passage which tells us the great truth about the love of God also speaks of condemnation and wrath. How foolish and superficial we are in our evangelism to emphasize either God's love or his wrath to the exclusion of the other. You can't have the one without the other. Love and wrath are but two sides of the same coin. God is both our Father and our Judge.

God's love is universal and personal. As someone has well said, "He loves each of us as if there was only one of us, and he loves all of us as he loves each of us." But his wrath is also universal and personal. "He who believes in the Son has eternal life; he who does not obey the Son shall not see life, but the wrath of God rests upon him" (v. 36).

We would do well to meditate upon the meaning and employment of these biblical dualities in our evangelism. Their proper use may help us through some troubled waters, and especially in the message which we share.

The Kingdom Concept in Evangelism

A fourth major point to learn from the case of Nicodemus is that the kingdom of God concept plays a major role in evangelism. While John's Gospel tends to use euphemisms such as "eternal life" for the kingdom of God, the phrase "kingdom of God" is actually used twice here (see vv. 3 and 5). Interestingly enough, we see both the actual phrase and one of its euphemisms, "eternal life" (see vv. 15-16).

Probably the first question put to Jesus by Nicodemus had to do with entrance into the kingdom of God. Every devout person in those days seems to have been talking about the kingdom of God, the *rule* of God, the *reign* of God, God's *government*, the domain where God is King and boss. Jesus himself had more to say about the kingdom of God than any other subject. His miracles were signs pointing to the presence and reality of the kingdom in his own life and ministry. His parables were mostly stories about the kingdom of God. One can never hope to understand our Lord's miracles or his parables apart from some comprehension of the phrase, "the kingdom of God."

So, Nicodemus wanted to know how he could become a citizen of God's kingdom. Probably William T. Sleeper was right when he said, "A ruler once came to Jesus by night, To ask Him the way of salvation and light." In other words, Nicodemus wanted to know how he could possess eternal life.

The answer of Jesus indicates that the kingdom of God can be *seen* and *entered* only through the door of the new birth. "Truly, truly, I say to you, unless one is born anew, he cannot see the kingdom of God" (v. 3). Moreover, "Truly, truly, I say to you, unless one is born of water and the Spirit, he cannot enter the kingdom of God" (v. 5).

Georgia Harkness, a United Methodist theologian reflecting on the kingdom of God, says, "I do not find the phrase 'to enter the kingdom' being used much these days, a discussion of the kingdom being centered mainly on the future when such discussion is carried on."[5] The case of Nicodemus should encourage us to give more attention to entrance into the kingdom in our evangelism.

Granted that the kingdom is future; it is also present; and one may enter it only through a spiritual metamorphosis called the new birth. Eternal life is not merely for the future, it is also for the present. Evangelism is being a midwife to the work of the Holy Spirit, birthing persons into the kingdom of God.

Notes
1. The Revised Standard Version of John 7:50 does not use the word *night*, but the King James Version does.

2. See G. Campbell Morgan, *The Gospel According to John* (Westwood, NJ: Fleming H. Revell Co., n.d.), p. 57.

3. See William James, *The Varieties of Religious Experience* (New Hyde Park, NY: University Books, 1902).

4. See Gabriel Fackre, *Word in Deed: Theological Themes in Evangelism* (Grand Rapids: Wm. B. Eerdmans, Publishing Co., 1975), pp. 32-36. See also Gabriel Fackre, *The Christian Story* (Grand Rapids: Wm. B. Eerdmans, Publishing Co., 1978), esp. pp. 41-51.

5. Georgia Harkness, *Understanding the Kingdom of God* (Nashville: Abingdon Press, 1974), p. 139.

5

The Woman at the Well
Zechariah 13:1; John 4:4-42

The case of the woman at the well is another example of Jesus knowing what was in persons. It is exhibit B of John 2:25. Jesus could read persons much as you and I might read a book. Whether his knowledge of persons was due to his divinity or to his highly sensitive intuition, you may decide for yourself. I would ascribe it more to his perfect humanity, rather than to his perfect divinity. Jesus was the only perfect human being who ever lived. Therefore, I do not think it strange for his human powers to be so highly developed that he could read a person's character.

The woman of Samaria is another representative person. Her story is related in keeping with John 20:30-31, "Now Jesus did many other signs in the presence of the disciples, which are not written in this book; but these are written that you may believe that Jesus is the Christ, the Son of God, and that believing you may have life in his name."

One other point which we might make by way of introduction is that the case of the woman at the well is used by more writers as a model for evangelism than any other story. More gold on evangelism is mined from this case than even from the case of Nicodemus. Indeed, John 4:4-42 may be the single most pregnant passage on witnessing in the whole Bible.

There are seven words which may be lifted up to help us mine some of the gold in this case. Those words are: customs, context, contact, content, confusion, continuity, and confirmation.

Customs

The case of the woman at the well shows us that Jesus broke some of the sacred customs and traditions of his day in order to save persons. We see Jesus breaking at least four customs and traditions in John 4:4-42.

First, he broke one custom by going through Samaria. Self-respecting Jews did not journey through Samaria when they traveled from Judea in the south to Galilee in the north. Even though most travel in the first century was on foot, or at best on donkey or horseback, most Jews would take the longer route, cross over the Jordan River at Jericho, travel up the east side of the Jordan, and cross over into Galilee only when they had completely bypassed Samaria. They took the more arduous route because they did not wish to be contaminated by the Samaritans.

Note, however, that the Scripture says of Jesus, "He had to pass through Samaria" (v. 4). This was a kind of divine appointment. Evidently, there was something *providential* about our Lord's journey through Samaria. Certainly it was an *intentional* act on his part. Could our Lord's mission through Samaria on this occasion have been a forerunner of Philip's mission in Acts 8?

Second, another custom is broken when Jesus asked the Samaritan woman for a drink of water, "Give me a drink" (v. 7). The woman was startled, and replied, "How is it that you, a Jew, ask a drink of me, a woman of Samaria?" (v. 9). A brief commentary by the author of the Fourth Gospel says, "For Jews have no dealings with Samaritans" (v. 9). That is to say, they have no social intercourse with each other. Jews and Samaritans kept their distance from each other. They kept as much physical and social distance from one another as they could. Not so Jesus, "the Savior of the world" (v. 42).

A third tradition is shattered by Jesus in John 4:24 when he said, "God is spirit, and those who worship him must worship in spirit and truth." It was traditional and customary for Jews to argue that persons ought to worship God on Mount Zion in Jerusalem and for Samaritans to argue that persons ought to worship God on Mount Gerizim. However, Jesus shattered both of those concepts, "Woman, believe me, the hour is coming when neither on this mountain nor in Jerusalem will you worship the Father" (v. 21).

I recall how a student asked me one day after class, "Why did you begin your prayer with the words, 'Eternal Spirit?'" That student was in his fifties and had never heard God addressed as "Eternal Spirit." Yet, Jesus said to the Samaritan woman, "God is spirit." He is not to be worshiped in any one place or sanctuary but in every place, because he is Spirit and is everywhere all the time.

A fourth custom which Jesus broke was in talking with a woman in public. Look at verse 27, "Just then his disciples came. They marveled that he was talking with a woman, but none said, 'What do you wish?' or, 'Why are you talking with her?'" They marveled not because of her nationality or character but because of her sex. "There is a rabbinical saying, 'A man should hold no conversation with a woman in the street, nor even with his own wife, still less with any other woman, lest men should gossip.'"[1]

See how Jesus broke the sacred customs and traditions of his day in his evangelism. If ever there was an iconoclast in evangelization, it was Jesus. Jesus cared more for persons than he did for foolish conventionalities which blasted human life. It was Jesus who said, "The sabbath was made for man, not man for the sabbath" (Mark 2:27).

When Ralph Neighbour was pastor of the West Memorial Baptist Church in Houston, Texas, he and the church members broke some customs and traditions of society in order to evangelize the night people of their city.[2] Christians are not supposed to go into bars, we are told. But suppose you go there to meet sinners on their turf, so that you might seek and save the lost? Perhaps some of us ought to at least entertain the possibility that there may be some sacred customs and traditions in our society which we shall have to break for the sake of persons who are of infinite worth and value.

Are you hamstrung in your evangelism by the traditions and customs of the elders? Or, are you an iconoclast in your evangelism like Jesus?

Context

This case also tells us something about the context of evangelism.

Evangelism never occurs in a vacuum but always in a specific physical and cultural context.

The physical context for this evangelistic encounter was out-of-doors, beside a well, under the wide-open sky. Jacob's well was a place of history and a source of refreshment. We are told that the well was probably over a hundred feet deep, and had a shaft seven and one-half feet wide.[3]

Can we not see in the very physical context for this conversion: (1) the suitability of doing evangelism in the out-of-doors; (2) the possibility of doing evangelism at a historical shrine; and, (3) the way many persons (including lost persons) are attracted to a place of refreshment such as a common well? Do you think it was *accidental* that Jesus encountered the woman of Samaria at such a place? I rather think it was *intentional* and premeditated on his part.

This is also an example of cross-cultural evangelism. The cultural context was that of first-century Samaria. Jesus thus shows us that we can witness to those who are different than we. Christian Jews can evangelize lost Samaritans. We can and must be witnesses to today's Samaritans and other races of our time and place.

Philip in Acts 8 crossed racial, social, and religious barriers when he led Samaritans and the Ethiopian eunuch to Christ (see vv. 4-40). What Jesus did, Philip did. What Jesus and Philip did, you and I can do also.

Perhaps there are three clues in this passage as to why we are not more effective in evangelizing across the barriers of race and religion and morals. First, we may not be sensitive enough to the great discovery that evangelism absolutely never occurs in a vacuum, but always in a specific physical, cultural, and spiritual context. Second, we may have never entertained the idea that evangelizing can be done outside of any building, under the sun or the stars. Third, we may be prejudiced against others because of their race or morals or sex.

Contact

The case of the woman at the well also tells us something about contact in our evangelism. Jesus had a natural point of contact with the woman. He asked a favor of her. He had no bucket or rope, but he did have a thirst for water, and that need became his point of contact with the woman. Physical water became his contact to tell her about the water of life.

One thing which Jesus and the woman had in common was their humanity. All human beings need water in order to satisfy their thirst. The fact that both of them needed water became their point of contact. There must be a point of contact with sinners, if we are to evangelize them. Often, our point of contact is at the level of basic needs for food, water, clothes, shelter, security, and so forth. This is what George Hunter calls "an Inductive-Grace model."[4]

At other times our point of contact is at the level of higher needs such as self-esteem, esteem for others, self-actualization, the desire to know and understand, and even aesthetic needs. Hunter labels this "an Inductive Mission model."[5]

Hunter goes so far as to suggest that the deductive model, which offers a general gospel and calls for an umbrella commitment to that general good news, "is no longer indigenous to the mental processes of many American peoples and sub-cultures." In fact, he cites England's Donald Lord Soper as saying, "We must begin where persons are, rather than where we would like for them to be." By that Soper means to say that the point of contact between persons and the gospel is their needs, hopes, yearnings, fears, longings, and deepest motives.[6]

Let us be very clear as to what a point of contact does not mean in evangelism. As a boy I listened regularly to a religious radio program. The preacher exhorted his hearers to find a point of contact while he prayed for them. That point of contact might even be simply laying your hand on the radio. Whatever we may say about the psychology of such a point of contact in a healing service, when we urge a point of contact in evangelism we do not mean literally a point of physical contact. Magic and sleight of hand have no place whatever in the evangelism of Jesus.

Abraham Maslow's hierarchy of needs may give us some pegs around which to hang what has been said concerning a point of contact in evangelism. According to Maslow a person's basic needs are physiological such as nutrition, elimination, sex, and sleep. Closely allied with such rock-bottom needs are safety needs such as security, stability, freedom from fear, anxiety, and chaos. Only when these lower needs are met may we be motivated by higher needs such as love and belongingness, esteem and self-actualization. I know of no writer on evangelism who has so effectively tied the point of contact to Maslow's hierarchy as has George Hunter.[7]

Content

This case tells us something about the content of evangelism. The content of our Lord's evangelism arose out of the situation. He suited his message to meet the needs of the individual with whom he was dealing. For example, to Nicodemus the highborn intellectual of Israel, Jesus said, "You must be born anew" (John 3:7). Yet there is no record he said exactly that to anyone else. That was the message which Nicodemus needed most to hear.

Another example is what he said to the rich young ruler, "If you would be perfect, go, sell what you possess and give to the poor, and you will have treasure in heaven; and come, follow me" (Matt. 19:21). There is no record he said that to anyone else.

That same procedure was followed with the woman of Samaria. She came to draw water. Jesus struck up a conversation with her about living water. This woman had a thirst which the water of this world had never been able to quench. Hence, "If you knew the gift of God, and who it is that is saying to you, 'Give me a drink,' you would have asked him and he would have given you living water" (v. 10).

See how naturally Jesus moved from physical water to living water. Living water is running water in contrast with rainwater. This living water is "the gift of God" (see v. 10). It is living in the sense that it is true to type, spiritual, eternal water. Apparently, it is the spontaneous energy of unfailing interior grace, "The water that I shall give him will become in him a spring of water welling up to eternal life" (v. 14).

Later Jesus puts the same truth a bit differently, "He who believes in me, as the scripture has said, 'Out of his heart shall flow rivers of living water' " (John 7:38). Therefore, let those who thirst come to Jesus and drink. We are told in the commentary by the fourth evangelist that Jesus was referring to the Holy Spirit (see John 7:39).

This living water which Jesus offered to the woman brings eternal satisfaction; whereas, in contrast, physical water only temporarily satisfies one's thirst. See how his content arose out of the context and the situation.

Furthermore, what Jesus said about spiritual worship and his messiahship arose out of the woman's comments (see vv. 19-26). He followed her lead in those two subjects.

We would do well to pattern our evangelism after Jesus in respect to its content. Our content should arise out of our context at the time. We, too, should learn to move from the natural to the spiritual in our message. We should suit out message to the unique needs of the persons with whom we deal. Whatever this world and its religions offer, we Christians have more and better to offer.

Please notice that while this woman's sex life sounded more like Hollywood today than Samaria in the first century, Jesus does not lecture her on her sexual sins. The content of his message did not stoop to such condemnation and abuse. Jesus was not a negative preacher who sought to build himself up by tearing others down. He let her know that he knew all about her sexual looseness and failures, but that was not the major thrust of his message. No, this evangelist had good news about living water, spiritual worship, and the Anointed One of God.

Confusion

The case of the woman at the well tells us something about confusion in evangelism. The woman was confused that a Jew would ask a drink of a Samaritan (see v. 9). Rabbi Eliezer ben Hyrcanus in the early second century said, "He that eats the bread of the Samaritans is like to one that eats the flesh of swine."[8]

She was also confused about the meaning of living water, "Sir, give me this water, that I may not thirst, nor come here to draw" (v. 15). Such confusion is characteristic of John's Gospel. Jesus makes a statement, then it is misunderstood. Remember how Nicodemus was confused about his statement concerning the new birth? "How can a man be born when he is old? Can he enter a second time into his mother's womb and be born?" (John 3:4).

This confusion expresses itself in terms of taking literally what Jesus had intended figuratively or spiritually. This may be an example of what Paul said in 2 Corinthians 2:14, "The unspiritual man does not receive the gifts of the Spirit of God, for they are folly to him, and he is not able to understand them because they are spiritually discerned." It may also be a teaching device which the fourth evangelist chose to use. Whatever the reason for such confusion, we should be forewarned that there will be confusion and lots of it in our evangelism. Persons will misunderstand our message. Both our style and substance may confuse them. Therefore, we should be prepared to clear up the confusion which we shall encounter.

Some confusion may be unavoidable because we are dealing with unsaved people, and spiritual truths require the Holy Spirit to interpret them. However, we can learn to be patient with such confusion, as was Jesus. Patiently and lovingly, line upon line and precept upon precept, Jesus sought to clear up the confusion which persons expressed. Somehow, he was always able to move his hearers from the literal to the deeper meaning.

Continuity

Now, we come to another Gibraltar-type truth in this case, namely to the importance of continuity in evangelism. The case lifts up four points of continuity which ought to characterize evangelism. First, there is a definite continuity between the work of evangelism and the will of God, the Father. We see that in John 4:31-34.

If evangelism is not the work dearest to our Father's heart, it is at least work so dear to his heart that through it he replenishes our faltering strength. Listen, "Meanwhile the disciples besought him, saying, 'Rabbi, eat.' But he said to them, 'I have food to eat of which you do not know.' So the disciples said to one another, 'Has any one brought him food?' Jesus said to them, 'My food is to do the will of him who sent me, and to accomplish his work' " (vv. 31-34).

When the Son evangelized, he was doing the will of the Father. And by implication, when all the sons and daughters of God evangelize, they are doing the will of the Father. You may be awfully hungry and thirsty and tired, but I know of nothing which will refresh you so quickly as to participate in the birth of a person into the kingdom of God.

Again, we see the truth of those words, "Man shall not live by bread alone, but by every word that proceeds from the mouth of God" (Matt.

4:4). To see a soul born into the kingdom of God right before our eyes, and especially when in response to our personal witness, will make us soar like an eagle and as bold as a lion. We need that kind of continuity in our evangelism.

Second, the case shows us the continuity between sowing and reaping in evangelism. "Do you not say, 'There are yet four months, then comes the harvest'? I tell you, lift up your eyes, and see how the fields are already white for harvest. He who reaps receives wages, and gathers fruit for eternal life, so that sower and reaper may rejoice together. For here the saying holds true, 'One sows and another reaps' " (vv. 35-37).

Sowing and reaping are intimately tied together in evangelism. Unless someone sows, there will be nothing to reap. He who sows will eventually reap. And, if perchance, sower and reaper are different persons, they can still rejoice together because the fruit has been gathered. There should be no discontinuity between the sower and the reaper in gathering the evangelistic harvest.

A third continuity is singled out in the case. There is a continuity with those who have labored faithfully before us. "For here the saying holds true, 'One sows and another reaps.' I sent you to reap that for which you did not labor; others have labored, and you have entered into their labor" (vv. 37-38).

This continuity in evangelism with those who have labored ahead of us, explains how it is that we may lead total strangers to Christ. We must never assume that we are the only laborers whom God has in his vineyard. Occasionally, we are permitted to lead persons to Christ within a few minutes because the saving word has already been sown in their hearts by others.

It is this kind of continuity in evangelistic work which accounts for the words of Paul in 1 Corinthians 3:6-8, "I planted, Apollos watered, but God gave the growth. So neither he who plants nor he who waters is anything, but only God who gives the growth. He who plants and he who waters are equal, and each shall receive his wages according to his labor."

A fourth continuity lifted up is our continuity with those who will labor behind us. Immediately, following the woman's conversion, she witnessed to others. "Many Samaritans from that city believed in him because of the woman's testimony, 'He told me all that I ever did' " (v. 39).

It is the divine intention that when we witness to persons and they are saved, those will in turn witness to others and thus pass on the faith. Hence, this continuity with those who follow in our witnessing train may be the most important continuity of the four. It is this continuity which leads to spiritual addition, reproduction, and multiplication as called for by Paul in 2 Timothy 2:2.

Confirmation

Last but not necessarily least, the case tells us that Jesus always confirms our testimony to him, if indeed it is a faithful and true testimony. Jesus confirmed the woman's testimony. "So when the Samaritans came to him, they asked him to stay with them; and he stayed there two days. And many more believed because of his word. They said to the woman, 'It is no longer because of your words that we believe, for we have heard for ourselves, and we know that this is indeed the Savior of the world' " (vv. 40-42).

We need to remember that Jesus is better than we are, and more than we. Whenever our testimony leads persons to Jesus, he will always confirm that testimony. While we are servants of Jesus, we can never be substitutes for him. If we can but bring persons to the feet of Jesus, he will keep them there. The proof of the pudding is in the eating. "O taste and see that the Lord is good!" (Ps. 34:8).

This case may also confirm four other truths in evangelization. The woman witnessed to those who knew her, as did Legion. Her life-style was known to all. She practiced at-home evangelism.

Her coming to draw water at that particular hour, "the sixth hour," was a kind of divine appointment for her as well as for Jesus. She came at precisely the same hour as did Jesus. God knows how to mesh schedules together. This was "one divine moment" for her. We see confirmed in this incident how chronological time can become pregnant with eternity!

Again, have you noticed the spontaneity of the woman's witnessing? Perhaps we don't share as eagerly and as spontaneously as did she because the quality of our experience is not the same. Does the case not confirm that motivation is a greater problem in witnessing than is methodology? Those who want to share Christ with others will find a way. If our "want to" is strong enough, we shall somehow discover the "how to." Motivation in evangelism is usually the mother of methods.

Notes

1. Cited by Wilbert F. Howard in *The Interpreter's Bible,* Vol. VIII (Nashville: Abingdon Press, 1952), pp. 529-30.
2. See Ralph W. Neighbour, Jr., and Cal Thomas, *Target-Group Evangelism* (Nashville: Broadman Press, 1975), esp. pp. 38-45. Neighbour found that "40 percent of all discussion in taverns concerns GOD!" (p. 38).
3. See Howard, p. 520.
4. George Hunter III, *The Contagious Congregation* (Nashville: Abingdon, 1979), pp. 45-48.
5. Ibid., pp. 48-50.
6. Ibid., pp. 38-39.
7. Ibid., pp. 35-63, and esp. pp. 41-44.
8. Quoted by Howard, p. 522.

6

An Official
Whose Son Was Ill

2 Kings 5:1-27; John 4:46-54

Look with me now at the case of an official whose son was ill. It so happens that this case is tied to one of a number of miracles of healing performed by Jesus.

That introduces us to two new elements in these case studies on the evangelism of Jesus, the elements of miracle and healing in conjunction with salvation. If you believe in the incarnation, what C. S. Lewis called "The Grand Miracle,"[1] you will probably not have any problem with these lesser miracles in our Lord's evangelism.

Salvation in the Bible is to be understood wholistically in terms of deliverance of the whole person in all of his or her relationships. Hence, the miracles of healing are part and parcel of the evangelism of Jesus. The healing of persons' bodies is never foreign, or extraneous, to our Lord's practice of evangelism. He is the Savior of our bodies as well as of our minds and spirits.

We have become so specialized in our understanding of soul and body that we altogether too readily relegate persons' bodies to the various secular health professions, so long as they will consent to let us deal with their souls. The medical profession has so refined their specialties that Sweden has no hospital which can deal with the whole body.

If you have only a liver problem, you can get the best care in the world in Sweden. But, if you simultaneously have a lung problem and a heart problem, there is no place where you can get the wholistic care which you need. I am thankful to see a renewed emphasis on the family and general practice of medicine in America. Also, I am grateful to see pastors and churches who believe that Jesus Christ saves our bodies as well as our souls.

Man's Extremity, God's Opportunity

The case of the official whose son was ill shows us again that mankind's extremity is still often God's opportunity in evangelism. "So he came again to Cana in Galilee, where he had made the water wine. And at Capernaum there was an official whose son was ill" (v. 46).

This man was desperate. His son was sick, to the point of death. He was at the end of his rope, and therefore desperate for help from any quarter.

Some persons turn to Jesus because they have nowhere else to go. Look for example at a witnessing experience related by one of my students. This happened in 1973 when he was a senior in college. A freshman by the name of Rush roomed on the same floor with him. They developed an acquaintance with each other. The senior began to witness to the freshman when he informed him that he was not a Christian.

Soon, the senior found out that Rush was on drugs. He began to pray daily for him. His verbal attempts to share with Rush seemed to get nowhere.

Rush's problem with drugs became acute. One afternoon as the senior returned to his room, there was a note on his bed from Rush. It said, "I need your help now." A hundred things rushed through the senior's mind as he made his way immediately to Rush's room.

Rush had been crying. The senior inquired about the note. At that point Rush began to pour out his heart to him. He had come to see that he had a drug problem that was getting worse every day. He wanted to quit, but he couldn't.

The senior told Rush that Christ could deliver him from his drug habit and give him peace and satisfaction that drugs could never offer. Rush kept saying that he didn't understand how this "Man" born two thousand years ago could help him. This perceptive senior said to him something like Philip told Nathanael, "Come and see" (John 1:46).

Finally, having no other place to turn, Rush, with many tears and a great gust of emotion, cried out to God for help and asked Christ to save him.

While the two of them were praying, the presence of God became so real and illuminating in that room that it was as if someone had turned on a hundred floodlights. Words cannot describe that moment. God's power delivered that young man from his bondage. Rush was set free from his habit and his sins. He now had Someone new upon whom he could depend.[2] Surely that was a case which illustrates how man's extremity often becomes God's opportunity.

Another of my students witnessed over a period of weeks to a big man who stood six feet two inches tall and weighed 275 pounds. The man's wife and four sons started coming to church. Later the mother and one boy transferred their church letters to that congregation. Shortly thereafter, one of the other sons became a Christian and was baptized into the body of Christ.

Still the father was not interested. It was like talking to a stone wall to try to witness to him. He told the student pastor, "I'm not interested in what you are saying, preacher."

Then, one morning tragedy struck that family. One of the boys was run over by an automobile and killed instantly while he was crossing the road in front of his house. When the preacher visited to comfort the family, the father met him at the door. Many people were present. The man said to the pastor, "How can I be saved?" They went into a back bedroom in order to talk privately. This young and faithful pastor shared with the grief-stricken father how he could become a Christian. They got down on their knees to pray as the big, broken man invited Jesus to come into his heart.[3] Certainly in that case man's extremity became God's opportunity.

Mother Teresa of India tells of a woman whom she picked out of a garbage bin. The lady was burning up with a fever and actually dying at that moment. She kept on saying, "My son did this to me!" She did not think of her sickness or pain or burning fever. No. "My son did this to me!"

Mother Teresa took the woman to her home for the dying where many hours were spent to ease her pain. She received the most gentle and tender loving care. Before she died, the lady said, "I forgive . . . my son."[4] While anger is sometimes stronger than sickness and hunger and pain, love is always stronger than hate.

Man's extremity is sometimes God's opportunity. Nor is that true only of individuals; it is also true of nations.

Leck Walesa, who was catapulted to the leadership of labor in Poland, was once asked whether communism had failed in his country. Walesa, as part of his answer, said:

They wanted us not to believe in God, and our churches are full. They wanted us to be materialistic and incapable of sacrifices; we are antimaterialistic, capable of sacrifice. They wanted us to be afraid of tanks, of the guns, and instead we don't fear them at all.[5]

The Plight of Our Children

A second point lifted up is that the plight of our sons and daughters sometime sends us parents to Jesus. "When he heard that Jesus had come from Judea to Galilee, he went and begged him to come down and heal his son, for he was at the point of death" (v. 47).

Dorothy Day, for example, felt compelled to join the Catholic Church after her daughter was born. Day felt such indescribable joy and gratitude that she said:

The final object of this love and gratitude was God. No human creature could receive or contain so vast a flood of love and joy as I felt after the birth of my child. With this came the need to worship, to adore.[6]

That decision to become a Christian required Day to give up the father of her child. He was an atheist, and they were living out of wedlock. "It was a simple question of whether I chose God or man," said Day.[7]

An old Japanese saying names the four most awful things on earth as fires, earthquakes, thunderbolts, and fathers! Fathers are awful at times, but I should hardly place them along with fires, earthquakes, and thunderbolts. Surely this sick boy's father demonstrates how deeply some fathers love their children, and to what extent they will go to help them.

However, it isn't only the sickness of our children and the indescribable love which we have for them which drives us to Jesus; we are more frequently driven to Jesus these days because of the sins of our children. When life caves in for our children because of their bondage to drugs, illicit sex, nicotine, and the many other gods of this world, we are often driven into the arms of Jesus. We flee to him as a kind of last resort, remembering that he said, "Come to me, all who labor and are heavy laden, and I will give you rest" (Matt. 11:28).

Sons do not always follow the footsteps of their fathers. The father of the real Jesse and Frank James was a Baptist minister who founded churches and assisted with the founding of a Baptist college. We would do well to remember in the practice of our evangelism that mankind's extremity is often God's opportunity, and that sometimes the plight of their children drives parents toward the arms of Jesus. Our children are our crown jewels, the most precious possessions given to us by God. Both their joys and their sorrows draw us to Jesus, who always makes our joy greater than our sorrow.

Surprise Signs

Dostoevski's Grand Inquisitor accused Jesus of thinking too highly of persons because he refused to help support their faith with the security of signs. Yet, a third point which the case of an official whose son was ill presents to us is that signs are sometimes given to those who do not seek them. This man was not interested in signs and wonders. All he wanted was for his boy to live.

Look at the text more closely, "Jesus therefore said to him, 'Unless you see signs and wonders you will not believe.' The official said to him, 'Sir, come down before my child dies' " (vv. 48-49).

Yet, we are told, "This was now the second sign that Jesus did when he had come from Judea to Galilee" (v. 54). I call this "the one o'clock sign" (see vv. 52-53). Jesus had said to the official at the seventh hour, or at 1:00 PM, "Go; your son will live" (v. 50). When his servants met him the next day and told him that his son was living, he inquired of them at what hour the boy had begun to mend. They said, "Yesterday at the seventh hour the fever left him" (v. 52). Then, the "father knew that was the hour when Jesus had said to him, 'Your son will live' " (v. 53).

Therefore, at the very hour when the father was told that his son would live, he began to mend. That one o'clock sign became a pivotal point in the story, although the man did not seek a sign.

Serendipity is the word we use to describe such surprises. How characteristic of Jesus to give us more than we ask. The father not only got healing for his son; he got a surprise sign to boot. When Jesus does something for a person, he does it well. There is often an unexpected plus in his gifts to us.

I warn you to look out for the element of surprise in your evangelism. God is full of surprises. He is the God of surprise. Did he not say to Moses, "I AM WHO I AM" (Ex. 3:14), or "I will be what I will be"?

Role of Belief in Salvation

This case teaches us something about the role of belief in salvation. Jesus said to him, "Unless you see signs and wonders you will not believe" (v. 48). But, the father did put credence in the power of Jesus to heal his son, "Sir, come down before my child dies" (v. 49).

When Jesus said, "Go; your son will live," we are told that "the man believed the word Jesus spoke to him and went his way" (v. 50). So, at first the official's faith was mere credence. Apparently his credence took a giant step from verse 49 to verse 50. Progress in the man's faith as mere credence is represented between his belief that Jesus could come down and heal his son in person, and that Jesus could speak the word and heal his son without actually being there physically.

Finally, we see a third forward movement in the official's belief in verse 53, "And he himself believed, and all his household." His faith had progressed from credence in the power of Jesus (vv. 48-49), to credence in the power of the word of Jesus (v. 50), to trust and commitment to Jesus as the Lord and Savior of himself and his family (v. 53).

Frequently, faith progresses like that in our practice of evangelism. Persons will move from one level of belief as credence to a deeper level of credence. Then, their faith will progress to the point where they trust Jesus to save them from their sins.

Please note that Jesus does not condemn such faith. On the contrary, he accepts and even rewards it. Both credence and trust are necessary elements in saving faith. The devils believe and tremble, but their belief is never more than mere credence. They believe the facts, but they remain devils because their faith has not the transforming power of trust and commitment.

I can believe that a chair will hold me up and support my body without crashing to the floor; but unless and until I actually trust myself to that chair by actually sitting down in it, my faith in the chair is mere credence, not trust. The same analogy holds for our faith in Jesus. We may believe intellectually that he is the Savior of the world; but, unless and until we trust ourselves to Jesus Christ to actually save us from our sins, our faith remains mere credence, not trust.

When John Paton translated the Scriptures for the South Sea Islanders, he discovered no word in their vocabulary for "believe," "trust," or "have faith." Finally one day a native came rushing into Paton's hut and thrust himself into a chair. The native said to Paton, "It's so good to rest my whole weight in this chair." That word which meant "resting one's whole weight upon" became Paton's word for faith.[8]

This distinction between faith as credence and trust is not a game with words. The distinction is extremely vital in evangelism. Both credence and trust are important ingredients of saving faith. We are not out to get persons simply to give intellectual consent to a set of facts about Jesus Christ.

Facts do not ultimately save a person, not even true facts about the Son of God. We are out to get persons to trust and commit themselves to Jesus Christ as their personal Lord and Savior. It is Jesus who saves and not belief in a set of facts about Jesus.

The official's faith was noteworthy, anyway we cut it. How remarkable that such a man believed so deeply! Perhaps he was an officer of some king, or even a Roman centurion in the service of Herod the tetrarch. Whoever he was, his faith (even as mere credence) resulted in the healing and health of his beloved son who was sick unto death. More than that, the man's faith resulted in the salvation of himself and his whole household.

I can tell you this: whenever one inquires of you, "What must I do to be saved," you can say with certainty, "Believe in the Lord Jesus, and you will be saved, you and your household" (Acts 16:31).

Household Evangelism

A very strong point made by this case is that the man and all his household believed. "The father knew that was the hour when Jesus had said to him, 'Your son will live'; and he himself believed, and all his household" (v. 53). Michael Green calls this "Household Evangelism."[9] Thomas Wolf calls it "Oikos Evangelism."[10]

Prior to going farther into the ramifications of household evangelism, let us pause to observe that the surest way to get a man's family may be to get him. That would be true in almost every patriarchal society. While we may cite examples of children and grandchildren reaching their fathers and grandfathers for Christ, usually it is the other way around.

Even in our increasingly unisex society, which is now undergoing a great shift in sexual roles, the key to reaching many whole families for Christ and his church is the father and husband. Our strong Western individualism notwithstanding, the surest route toward winning a man's family is to win the man. Nevertheless, we tend to take the course of what we perceive to be the least resistance in our evangelism. We tend to go after the children and youth and wives prior to going after the symbolical head of the family.

Could it be that our whole strategy for evangelism needs to be rearranged in order to give priority to reaching the real, or at least the symbolical, head of the family? We need not totally accept the "trickle-down" theory of evangelism in order to follow this head-of-the-household strategy.

Do you know the "trickle-down" theory of evangelism? Here it is: "When I get Christ's vital message of the Kingdom of God to the king, president, prime minister and others high in the government of such nations, I have, in God's sight, gotten His message to that nation or kingdom." Those are the words of Herbert W. Armstrong, founder and Pastor General of The Worldwide Church of God.[11] That, too, was the theory of Frank Buchman's Moral Re-Armament.

Contrary to the "trickle-down" theory of evangelism, the head-of-the-household theory contends that we should reach the key person in that socioeconomic unit in order to effectively reach all of the other members of that entity. We can never claim that any household has been totally evangelized until all of its individual members hear and heed the message of the gospel.

Wolf calls this *oikos* evangelism because that is the Greek word for house or household. This official's household consisted of his wife, and children, and servants. What is your household? Is it not your circles of influence such as your immediate family, relatives, close friends, business associates, neighbors, acquaintances, and persons whom God may send across your path from time to time? Your particular sphere of existence is your household, your Jerusalem.

Let me hasten to say that you do not have to be the head of a household in order to practice *oikos* evangelism. Robert H. Culpepper has related the conversion experience of a Japanese Christian named Masao Kawaguchi which illustrates this. Kawaguchi had hated his father because he often came home drunk and abused his wife and children. That hatred was confessed to God and forgiven. At the time of his conversion, his father was in the hospital seriously ill. Kawaguchi rushed to the hospital and spoke pleadingly to the doctor: "Please don't let my father die. He's not saved yet." The doctor, of course, didn't know what he was saying. His father did recover. Though at first he did not understand what his son was trying to tell him, he could understand that his son's attitude toward him had radically changed. Before long, Kawaguchi had led all of his family to Christ—his father, his older sister, his two younger brothers, and his mother.[12] That, too, is household evangelism.

When you were saved, was your whole household saved? Do you want to see your household saved? Do you recognize that God is holding you responsible for witnessing to those in your circles of influence? Do you recognize and accept the fact that these deepest relationships in your household are your best witnessing opportunities? That is what is meant by household evangelism.

I confess that for a long time I neglected these New Testament references to the salvation of households. Perhaps I was afraid that they might contradict what I believed about believers' baptism by immersion. Subconsciously I am sure that I thought those who practiced infant baptism used such passages to buttress their arguments. So I just steered clear of them.

Reading Donald McGavran and the literature on the church growth movement forced me to take a new look at the Scriptures on household evangelism. This case in John 4 is only one of several.

Acts 16:15 tells us that Lydia "with her household" was baptized. Acts 16:31-33 tells us that the Philippian jailer and his household were converted and baptized. Lest you think that to be a slip of Luke's pen, three references to it are made in those three verses. "And they said, 'Believe in the Lord Jesus, and you will be saved, you and your household.' And they spoke the word of the Lord to him and to all that were in his house. And he took them the same hour of the night, and washed their wounds, and he was baptized at once, with all his family."

Then, too, there is a reference where an angel is reported to have told Cornelius, "Send to Joppa and bring Simon called Peter; he will declare to you a message by which you will be saved, you and all your household" (Acts 11:13-14). Therefore, we have at least these four examples where whole households were saved.

Jesus was the first to practice household evangelism. Both Paul and Peter followed his example. Should we not do likewise?

Role of Faith in Prayer for Salvation

This case also teaches us something about the role of faith in prayer for the salvation of persons. Jesus was begged to come down and heal the man's son. However, he healed the boy without going down. If the miracle which Jesus worked on this occasion was effectual across a distance of more than twenty-five miles, does not God have the power to cross any distance?

John Bunyan, in *Grace Abounding,* says one of the seven abominations still in his heart was that he had not watched for the answers to his prayers. Perhaps we do not need to remind ourselves that it is a monstrous discourtesy to ask one for a favor and then to go away without waiting for the answer. Jesus once said: "Whatever you ask in prayer, believe that you have received it, and it will be yours' " (Mark 11:24).

Some years back I knew a fourteen-year-old boy who was not a professing Christian. His parents were concerned about his salvation. They had talked to him specifically about his becoming a Christian. Their pastor had talked with him. All of his brothers and sisters, both older and younger, had confessed their faith in Christ and been baptized. His parents had begun to wonder if he would ever confess faith in Christ.

At that point, a furloughing missionary learned of the young man and his parents' concern for his salvation. The missionary assured the boy's father that he was going to pray in faith for the boy's salvation. Very shortly after the missionary started praying, the fourteen-year-old unexpectedly made a public confession of faith and was baptized. Call that coincidence if you choose, but it may well be a case of answered prayer.

Notes
1. See C. S. Lewis, *Miracles: A Preliminary Study* (New York: Association Press, 1958), pp. 77-93.
2. Related by Daniel Merritt in an unpublished paper titled, "My Most Unforgettable Witnessing Experience," in course number M4532, during the summer of 1981.
3. Related by Don Turner in a paper titled, "My Most Unforgettable Personal Witnessing Experience," in course number M4532, during the summer of 1981.
4. See Mother Teresa, "God's Understanding Love," *Seeds,* Vol. 4, No. 2, February, 1981, p. 8.
5. Oriana Fallaci, "Walesa Just a 'Hungry Hare' Following No Specific Ideology," *The Kansas City Times,* March 19, 1981, p. A-4.
6. Quoted by Nancy L. Roberts, "Building a New Earth: Dorothy Day and the 'Catholic Worker,' " *The Christian Century,* XCVII, No. 40, Dec. 10, 1980, p. 1217.
7. Ibid., p. 1218.
8. Related by John McArthur in *CMN Net Work,* Vol. 1, No. 3, March, 1981, p. 3.
9. See Michael Green, *Evangelism in the Early Church* (Grand Rapids: Wm. B. Eerdmans Publishing Co., 1970), pp. 207-223.

10. See Thomas A. Wolf, "Oikos Evangelism: Key to the Future," in Ralph W. Neighbour, Jr., compiler, *Future Church* (Nashville: Broadman Press, 1980) pp. 153-76.

11. Quoted by Dean M. Kelley in a book review of *Against the Gates of Hell* by Stanley R. Rader (Everest House) in *The Christian Century,* Vol. XCVII, No. 37, Nov. 19, 1980, p. 1136.

12. Robert H. Culpepper, *God's Calling: A Missionary Autobiography* (Nashville: Broadman Press, 1981), pp. 81-82.

7

The Man Who Had Been Ill for Thirty-Eight Years

Isaiah 55:1; John 5:1-18

There is some resemblance between this case and that of the paralytic borne by four in Mark 2:1-12. "Rise, take up your pallet, and walk" (v. 8), and the result, "He took up his pallet and walked" (v. 9), are one point of similarity. Another connection is the relation between physical and spiritual evil in both cases. To the paralytic Jesus said: "My son, your sins are forgiven," (Mark 2:5). To this man Jesus later says: "See, you are well! Sin no more, that nothing worse befall you" (v. 14).

Good Occasion to Evangelize

A feast is a good occasion to evangelize. Many who come to a feast to be filled are empty. Some lonely persons feel even more lonely during great holidays. Such may have been the case with those people at the pool of Bethzatha in Jerusalem.

While many celebrate on the great holidays, others cringe in fear and cry themselves to sleep. Loneliness is even less endurable during the great feasts of our society. Festival occasions almost always present excellent opportunities for faith sharing.

We can at such feasts feed the hungry with the bread of life. We can fill the thirsty with the water of life. We can at such times single out the lonely for special attention and consolation.

I recall that in 1973 a group of Christians decided to set up a witnessing tent at the South Carolina state fair. We were amazed at the number of persons who came in for free refreshments and honest dialogue. Some who came to see the sights, play the games, and ride the fast machines got more than that for which they paid. They got saved.

Humanity's Point of Need

Christ in his evangelism is to be found at humanity's point of need. Where would you expect to find Jesus in a feast like this? Would he be in the Temple, or at least out on the streets where everybody could see him? No. He was to be found at the place of the greatest need. Please note that Jesus took the initiative in seeking out this man.

We find him at the pool of Bethzatha where "lay a multitude of invalids, blind, lame, paralyzed" (v. 3). This was no pretty sight. How pitiful they must have been. My guess is that the odors were unpleasant and very foul. Nor are we told about their groanings and lamentations. Nevertheless, we can imagine that the sounds which filled the air were taxing on sensitive ears and compassionate hearts.

"I don't think anybody cares for me." Those words, or something quite like them, were reportedly the last words of Marilyn Monroe before she took an overdose of sleeping pills and went out into eternity. How remarkably like that are the words of Psalm 142:4, "No man cares for me." Have you ever felt like that?

Robert Schuller, founder and pastor of Garden Grove Community Church in Orange County, California, suggests to us that "the secret of a growing church is so simple—find the hurt and heal it."[1] Schuller spent some months going from door-to-door in Garden Grove inquiring about the needs of the people. His church self-consciously set out to meet those needs. For more than eighteen years Garden Grove grew at the incredible rate of more than 500 percent per decade.

There are too many sins of omission among us when it comes to finding and healing the hurts of humanity. Someone said to a little boy, "Son, do you know what the sins of omission are?" The boy said, "Yes sir, those are the sins we should have committed and didn't." Well, that's not quite right, is it?

A few years ago a man was found dead in a large southern city, one Christmas. The man was more than a week overdue with his rent. So they broke into his room to see what had happened to him. He had been dead for about ten days. Nobody had missed him. There were no clothes in his apartment, not even one additional change of garments. He had lived in that one room in abject poverty. No food, no clothes, emaciated. There was a note scribbled on a torn paper bag. Written with a pencil it said, "Nobody loves me. Nobody lo. . . ." That was the last word he said to the world.

Think of that. It happened in a city with many churches and great southern hospitality. It might have happened in your city or mine. The tragedy is that it happened.

God loved that man. But God's people did not incarnate that love so that the man could experience it and know it. And *agape* love is meeting the needs of persons.

The Reach of the Helping Hand

The case shows us that no one is beyond the reach of Christ's helping hand. Jesus selected the neediest case of all the cases gathered around the pool of Bethzatha. "One man was there who had been ill for thirty-eight years" (v. 5). This man had been paralyzed for thirty-eight years. That's longer than many have been in the world!

If we would learn to select some of the more difficult cases for our practice of evangelism, the power of the gospel might be authenticated quicker. Jesus can handle the most difficult cases we may bring to him.

Note that Jesus does not take the path of least resistance in his evangelism. Some of us are only attempting to win the children to Christ. Why not try to win the adults also? Some of us are concentrating on youth and women in our evangelism. Why not seek to win the men and the hardened veterans of Satan as well?

No one is beyond the reach of Christ's helping hand, not even those who are dead in trespasses and in sins. I have heard a reliable Christian leader tell about a local church in the south which turns in a church letter each year to its district association. Year after year that church reports no baptisms. And little wonder because it only has about twelve members. They meet only once every three months, and all they do when they meet together is clean their cemetery! So, there is a church which exists for the sole purpose of keeping up its cemetery.

I don't have anything against a church keeping up its cemetery. In fact, I am wholeheartedly for it. However, I do have problems with any church which exists solely to maintain its cemetery, don't you? A church which is only a keeper of its cemetery is no church.

A keeper of cemeteries! May God forbid that our churches shall degenerate to such a point that their only reason for existing is to care for the physically dead. Should it not be exactly the opposite? Should not the church exist primarily to raise the dead, to bring new life to those who are dead in trespasses and in sins? A church exists to raise the dead, not to bury the dead. Jesus said, "Let the dead bury their dead" (KJV).

Self-Will and Self-Image in Evangelism

Jesus in his evangelism puts a question to those who are "waiting for the moving of the water" (v. 3, KJV): "Do you want to be healed?" (v. 6).

Some 14,000 times that poor man may have sought to reach the healing waters! What a foolish question, you say. No, some folk enjoy being crippled. Some enjoy the sins of the flesh so much that they really and truly don't want to have the radical surgery which Christ requires.

"Want to" is necessary for salvation. A decision of the will is involved. We may not be whole because we do not want to be whole. We rather enjoy our incapacities, our weaknesses, our incompletion.

Gaines S. Dobbins saw this question giving the man a sense of "worthwhileness," the sense that someone cared for him![2] Self-image is important in evangelism. Also, self-will is vital to evangelism. To be saved, one must exercise his will as well as his emotions.

Hence, the question may have been a recognition of the man's worth and individuality. This is no idle, unimportant question, but central, and all important.

Studs Terkel of Chicago once started a conversation with his fellow patrons at a bar something like this: "I'm not too sure that absolute power corrupts absolutely. I think absolute powerlessness corrupts absolutely. I think to feel needed is terribly important."[3]

The Importance of a Friend

We also may see in this case the importance of a friend in evangelism. "Sir, I have no man to put me into the pool when the water is troubled, and while I am going another steps down before me" (v. 7).

This man could have never been healed without the help of a friend. The healing waters are waiting, but some will never be touched by them unless some friend helps them to Jesus.

Perhaps this long-term paralytic was not the kind to naturally attract friends. Evidently, he had gotten that way through some foolish act of sin in his youth (see v. 14). There was no beauty or attractiveness in him. Yet, Jesus befriended him. Jesus is the friend of all sinners. The songwriter was right: "No one ever cared for me like Jesus."

The experience of the Church of Jesus Christ of the Latter-Day Saints tells us something about the importance of friendship evangelism. When Mormon missionaries go from door-to-door, their conversion rate is .1 percent, or one in every 1,000 confrontations. However, if a Mormon friend or relative opens his home for a place where missionary contact occurs, the odds of success increase to 50 percent. The Mormons, in other words, have discovered that their best recruitment is done by their rank-and-file members as they build intimate interpersonal ties with non-Mormons and then link them into a Mormon social network.[4]

Bob Dylan, the most acclaimed songwriter of the rock era, was converted to Christ in 1978. His very successful album, "Slow Train Coming," told the story of his conversion. Two things stand out to me in Dylan's conversion. First, Dylan was not down and out when Christ became his Savior. "The funny thing is a lot of people think that Jesus comes into a person's life only when they are either down and out or they are miserable or just old and withering away," said Dylan. "That's not the way it was for me. I was doing fine."

A second thing which stands out about Dylan's conversion is the role a close friend played. "I was relatively content," said Dylan, "but a very close friend of mine mentioned a couple of things to me, and one of them was Jesus. Well, the whole idea of Jesus was foreign to me. I said to myself, 'I can't deal with that. Maybe later.' But later, it occurred to me that I trusted this person (the friend), and I had nothing to do the next couple of days so I called the person back and said I was willing to listen about Jesus.'"[5]

Friends are exceedingly important in evangelism. Let us learn to befriend those who have everything but friends, and those who have nothing including friends, in order to introduce them all to Jesus our friend, who is a friend to the friendless.

Iconoclasm in Evangelism

The sabbath was a sacred icon to many Jews in the days of Jesus. The Mishnah lists thirty-nine works which are forbidden on the sabbath. For example, it is allowed to carry a living man on a pallet on the sabbath, but not to carry the pallet itself.

See again in this case how Jesus broke the law of the sabbath in his evangelism. Jesus was an iconoclast in his evangelism. He smashed the traditions surrounding the sabbath, because he believed persons were more important.

An important clue to understanding the case of the man who had been ill for thirty-eight years is that it occurred on the sabbath day. Look at verses 9 and 10, "Now that day was the sabbath. So the Jews said to the man who was cured, 'It is the sabbath, it is not lawful for you to carry your pallet.' "

Actually verse 16 gives us an even better clue to the anger of the authorities toward Jesus. Williams translates John 5:16 as follows: "This is why the Jews were persecuting Jesus, because He persisted in doing such things on the sabbath." The imperfect tense is used, and neither the King James Version or the Revised Standard Version brings out its force.

These authorities may have reasoned that the man had been like that for thirty-eight years, what would another day have been to him? But they were dealing with the Lord of the sabbath.

Jesus is also Lord over us and our sacred traditions. His famous statement about the sabbath applies to other similar institutions, customs, and mores of any society: "The sabbath was made for man, not man for the sabbath" (Mark 2:27).

A Worse Consequence of Sin

There is a worse consequence of sin than thirty-eight years of paralysis. After the authorities had questioned the former paralytic,

Jesus found him and said, "See, you are well! Sin no more, that nothing worse befall you" (v. 14).

Can anything be worse than thirty-eight years of paralysis? Yes! "The wages of sin is death" (Rom. 6:23). Jesus said: "And do not fear those who kill the body but cannot kill the soul; rather fear him who can destroy both body and soul in hell" (Matt. 10:28).

The consequences of sin are dreadful and tragic. Sin persisted in results in what the Bible calls "the second death" (see Rev. 20:6; 21:8). Look, for example, at Revelation 21:8, "But as for the cowardly, the faithless, the polluted, as for murderers, fornicators, sorcerers, idolaters, and all liars, their lot shall be in the lake that burns with fire and sulphur, which is the second death."

I do not major on hell fire in my preaching. My preference is to preach on the love of God rather than the wrath of God. Nevertheless, I believe in the terrible reality of judgment and wrath. God must punish sin in order to protect his holiness. His wrath is the reverse side of his love.

Paul is right, "We must all appear before the judgment seat of Christ, so that each one may receive good or evil, according to what he has done in the body" (2 Cor. 5:10). The writer of Hebrews seems to have something like that in mind when he says, "It is appointed for men to die once, and after that comes judgment" (Heb. 9:27). In fact, the writer of John's Gospel sees God's wrath as already active in the world upon the children of disobedience (see John 3:36).

God does not send persons to hell. They send themselves there through their unbelief, rebellion, and shameful choices in this present life. We do ourselves, our fellowmen, and our God a great disservice when we refuse to warn persons to flee the wrath of God in our evangelizing.

The entrance into eternity is through time and space. At least that is true of all human beings. If we wish to get into heaven, we'll have to get heaven into us right here on earth. Heaven is a prepared place for a prepared people. You have to have the nature of God in your being in order to get into heaven.

Is the same condition true of outer darkness and that place the Bible calls hell? Surprise! Surprise! Hell may turn out to be an unprepared place for an unprepared citizenry. Hell may be the cosmic garbage dump of the universe. It resembles chaos and a completely unsupervised prison for criminals. But it too is entered through time and space. We reap in the afterlife what we sow in the present life.

We should lovingly and longingly and everlastingly speak this truth in love in our evangelism: There is a worse consequence of sin than thirty-eight years of physical paralysis. The ultimate consequence of sin is eternal separation from God and everlasting separation from our loved ones and friends who die in the Lord.

Then, there is a final footnote about sin in this case. We should not suppose that Jesus is reverting to the pre-Job era by connecting this man's paralysis with his sin. He emphatically did not believe or teach that all physical illness is caused by sin. But Job notwithstanding, some sickness of the body, the mind, and indeed the soul is caused by sin.

My personal opinion is that Jesus knew something about this man's past that you and I don't know, and about which the text is almost silent. I think this is another example of what is said in John 2:25 about Jesus knowing "all men" and not needing anyone to tell him those things which he already knew.

Evangelism Is Costly

A final point which I wish to lift up from this case is that evangelism is costly business. There is nothing cheap about biblical evangelism. It is an expensive enterprise. It cost Jesus his life.

That last part of the case in John 5:15-18 shows us how the enemies of Jesus persecuted him because he broke the laws of the sabbath. Those verses also point out that they sought to kill Jesus because he "called God his own Father, making himself equal with God" (v. 18). Those two charges of sabbath-breaking and claiming to be equal with God are examples of the kind of accusations which eventually led to his crucifixion.

We may need to speak more about the demands of the gospel. What does the good news demand? Well, for one thing it demands a response, a yes or no, acceptance or rejection. For another thing, the gospel demands repentance. It requires a revolutionary change in persons. It demands a profound metamorphosis in our life-style. The gospel demands that we become faithful disciples of Jesus Christ. No doubt that minister was sincere who said: "I like to think of myself as a Buddhist on Monday, a Hinduist on Tuesday, a Jew on Thursday and a Christian on Friday."[6] However, I disagree. I should like to think of every Christian as an everyday Christian and as an always Christian. The servant is never greater than his or her master in evangelism. The blood of the martyrs is still the seed of the church. There is always a cross in evangelism. As the hymn says:

> Must Jesus bear the cross alone,
> And all the world go free?
> No, there's a cross for ev'ryone,
> And there's a cross for me.

Notes

1. Robert Schuller, *Your Church Has Real Possibilities* (Glendale, CA: Regal Books, 1974), p. 4.

2. See Gaines S. Dobbins, *Evangelism According to Christ* (Nashville: Broadman Press, 1949), p. 61.

3. See "The Great American Ear," *Newsweek,* Oct. 13, 1980, p. 118.

4. See the editorial in *Church Growth: America,* Vol. 6, No. 5, Nov.-Dec., 1980, p. 2.

5. See Robert Hilburn's "Bob Dylan's Views on Christianity, or, 'Don't Think Twice, It's All Right,' " *The Kansas City Times,* Nov. 28, 1980, pp. E-1 and E-2.

6. See Mack Alexander, "He Takes Unitarians on a Wild Trip to Other Religions," *The Kansas City Times,* March 7, 1981, p. C-7.

8

The Man Born Blind

Isaiah 42:6-7; John 9:1-41

John's Gospel always balances the word and the deed. There is never a word in the Fourth Gospel without a corresponding deed. The case of the man born blind in John 9 is the deed which corresponds to the word of Jesus in John 8:12, "I am the light of the world; he who follows me will not walk in darkness, but will have the light of life." This case is a sign to illustrate that saying. John 9:5 further bears this out and connects this case with the saying, "I am the light of the world."

Another clue to the meaning of this miracle is the words of Jesus in verse 39, "For judgment I came into this world, that those who do not see may see, and that those who see may become blind." There is indeed a biblical sense in which evangelism is opening blind eyes and closing supposedly open eyes. Paul's commission on the Damascus road was stated in terms of opening blind eyes: "I send you to open their eyes, that they may turn from darkness to light and from the power of Satan to God" (Acts 26:17-18).

An Example of Impromptu Evangelism

The case of the man born blind is an example of impromptu evangelism, or witnessing which was apparently spontaneous and unpremeditated. John 9:1 tells us, "As he passed by, he saw a man blind from his birth." So much of the evangelism of Jesus occurred as "he passed by," or on the run so to speak. Other immediate examples which come to mind are the woman with an issue of blood (Mark 5:24-34), Matthew at the seat of custom (Matt. 9:9), the blind beggar of

Jericho (Luke 18:35-43), Zacchaeus (Luke 19:1-10), and the woman at the well (John 4:4-42).

Has God ever dumped an evangelistic opportunity into your lap? Evangelism is wherever you want to find it. Jesus found evangelistic opportunities as he passed by, and as he moved through certain places. His dealings with the woman at the well in Samaria illustrate that further. Evangelistic eyes see evangelistic opportunities almost everywhere.

Importance of Seeing in Evangelism

The case lifts up for us the importance of "seeing" in evangelism. Karl Barth even goes so far as to speak of Christian existence as "seeing clearly." Verse 1 tells us that Jesus saw a man blind from birth. The Greek verb indicates a deliberate gaze—not just a mere glance. Jesus really saw this man who had never seen anyone or anything. The man had never seen the light of day or the beauty of a fading sunset, but Jesus saw him and looked right into his heart.

J. H. Jowett somewhere comments that the eyes of Jesus never missed anything. He saw Nathanael under the fig tree. He saw Matthew at the seat of custom. He saw Zacchaeus up that sycamore tree. He saw the blind beggar beside the road outside of Jericho. He sees you and me. He sees and knows all.

There are at least three persons whom we need to really see in our evangelism. We need to see the blind beggars beside the roadsides of our world. D. T. Niles was right, evangelism is one beggar telling another beggar where to find bread. But if we fail to see the blind beggars beside every roadside, how shall we tell them that in Jesus Christ is the bread of life?

We also need to see ourselves in a true light, in the light of Christ. We need to see ourselves as God sees us so that we might think soberly of ourselves and not be haughty or puffed up with false pride.

We also need to see Jesus, our coach, the author and finisher of our faith. As the writer of Hebrews says: "Looking to Jesus the pioneer and perfecter of our faith, who for the joy that was set before him endured the cross, despising the shame, and is seated at the right hand of the throne of God" (12:2).

First John 1:1 speaks of the word of life as that "which we have seen with our eyes, which we have looked upon." Until we gaze upon Jesus and let his eyes penetrate our hearts, we can never truly see ourselves or others.

Theologizing in Evangelism

We may learn from this case something about theologizing in our evangelism. Verse 2 indicates that this case aroused the theological interest of the disciples: "Rabbi, who sinned, this man or his parents, that he was born blind?" The twelve seemed more concerned with the theological problem than with the man's real need.

There is nothing wrong with theologizing about cases in evangelism. The best time to reflect theologically on a case, however, is usually after the encounter rather than during it. A more appropriate time is during the debriefing.

While reflecting on this case from John 9, I had a witnessing encounter which further illustrated the above truth to me and to the two witnesses who went out with me. Our prospect was a man whom I shall call Don Spock, age fifty-three, and so far as we knew a lost man.

Remember now, there were three of us: myself, a layman in his thirties, and a teenage girl. When we rang the doorbell, two young boys came to the door. They went back and brought their mother. As she saw us standing outside in the semidarkness, her first words to us were: "My goodness, have you come to rob us?" I stepped back and said: "No, ma'am, we are from the Northgate Baptist Church." Then, I immediately introduced myself and the two who were with me. That disarmed her and gained us an invitation to come into the house.

Following some small talk about family and home, my prospect, Mr. Spock, came into the living room. He was staggering. His eyes were glazed. His speech was slow and his reflexes were definitely out of sync with that of a normally healthy person. I could tell that his eyes were heavy. My first impression was that this gentleman was either on alcohol or drugs, or that he was taking some kind of medication.

As we talked on, we learned that Mr. Spock had suffered a stroke a few years back, and more recently had a heart attack. He was at that moment under heavy medication. In fact, he had just returned from a lengthy treatment at the hospital.

We were surprised to learn that he was still holding down a full-time job. He had been a sales manager for a large company. Now, his sight was about gone. Nevertheless, his company thought so much of him, and he had such fierce pride in being able to support his wife and two children that he was still working, even though his wife had to chauffeur him to and from work.

I was struck by the comparative youth of his wife and two well-behaved sons. He told me with a sense of pride that his house and cars were paid for. They had enrolled their sons in a church school, in spite of the costly tuition. Never have I met a gentleman with a stronger sense of duty or with a greater determination to support his wife and children and not to be beholden to the government or to anybody.

The man was trying to live by the Golden Rule, without realizing that one cannot live by the ethics of the kingdom of God unless he is a citizen of that kingdom. He wanted what the church could offer his sons but did not see any inconsistency between that and his own refusal to turn his life over to God. We were able to commend him for his sense of duty, his diligent efforts to be self-supporting, his love for his wife and children, his upright character, and so forth. However, our hearts ached to see him acknowledge that God was his helper and healer and Savior.

Now, mind you all of this theological reflection came *after* our visit and not during it. We were too busy during the visit to think upon all of these important points in the theology of evangelism. When you are face-to-face with a blind man, you don't ask in that moment deep theological questions like: "Who sinned, this man or his parents, that he was born blind?"

It is always appropriate to theologize *following* a witnessing encounter. However, it is seldom, if ever, appropriate to theologize about a case when we are actually in the process of dealing with an individual or a family.

The Unexpected Answer in Evangelism

The unexpected answer in evangelism is also illustrated by this case. John 9:3 says: "It was not that this man sinned, or his parents, but that the works of God might be made manifest in him."

The common notion was that physical disability was the result of sin, Job notwithstanding. Jesus answered in effect, "Neither." This was the nontraditional answer by Jesus, the iconoclast.

The really important thing in evangelism is to make known the works of God, not to fix the blame for one's condition. Jesus was not nearly so concerned with fixing blame as he was with helping the needy person.

Has God ever surprised you with an answer to your theological problems in evangelism? Many years ago I read a book, the title of which has escaped me. The author told about a chaplain who went in to talk with a man on death row. That man had been condemned to die in an electric chair for crimes which he had committed. He had with him in his cell a small crucifix.

The chaplain, seeking to comfort the condemned man, pointed to the crucifix and said something like this: "You are not the only man to die. Jesus died too." "But, he died for a purpose," said the prisoner, "there is no purpose in my death." Like a flash of lightning the chaplain said he saw more clearly than ever before the difference between Christ's death and the death of all others. That encounter opened up to the chaplain the deeper meaning of Christ's crucifixion.

We can learn from living documents as well as from written documents in our evangelizing. Let us keep our ears tuned for the unexpected answer in our evangelistic encounters. We may learn something unexpected, either from the persons with whom we deal or from the Spirit who is our greatest teacher.

Urgency in Evangelism

A fifth element which the case of the man born blind lifts up for us is urgency in evangelism. Jesus said, "We must work the works of him who sent me, while it is day; night comes, when no one can work" (v. 4).

Note the plural "we." The disciples are included. You and I are included in that we. "We must work. . . ." See how this word of urgency picks up on "the works of God" in John 9:3.

Jesus is the sent one and so are we, "As the Father has sent me, even so I send you" (John 20:21). This note of urgency about the works of

God is sounded in a missionary context. The basic idea in the word *mission* is "sending." Jesus is the missionary, that is, the sent one, par excellence. Yet in a real and extended sense we too are missionaries, or sent ones.

Today we live and work in a missionary context. We are now persons under orders. Our mission is: "Let your light so shine before men, that they may see your good works and give glory to your Father who is in heaven" (Matt. 5:16). However, tomorrow the night may come. Our commission may cease. Judgment may fall. When this final night comes, this night of all nights, this curtain of darkness like that which enveloped the whole earth when our Lord was crucified, the mission will cease.

We do not have forevermore to evangelize those who sit in the blindness of darkness. There is an end time to all evangelism and missions. God will let down a cosmic curtain of darkness one day. And the long-awaited Day of the Lord will come, which will be a day of judgment for humankind and for all the nations of the earth.

Physical Elements in the Miracle

A sixth point which the case makes is that Jesus used physical elements in this man's healing. Spit, clay, and water are utilized. "He spat on the ground and made clay of the spittle and anointed the man's eyes with the clay, saying to him, 'Go, wash in the pool of Siloam' (which means Sent). So he went and washed and came back seeing" (vv. 6-7).

Modern medical science knows the value of physical elements in healing. Placebos are often used in medical experiments. These physical elements would aid the man's faith. Persons sometimes need assistance with their faith. Jesus is not opposed to the use of legitimate assistance.

Two other ideas present themselves in connection with the use of physical elements. There is a wordplay on the word *Sent*. The pool of Siloam means "Sent." Jesus, who refers to himself as "sent" by the Father, sends the blind man to the pool called "Sent." The startling result was that the healed man himself became a sent one, or a missionary, to others!

We can hardly escape the conclusion that every Christian is a blind person whom Jesus has sent to be baptized in a sending pool as it were, in order that he or she may in return become a sent one to others. Hence, the physical element of water has been used with us all in our baptism. Are we not all and each commissioned and ordained by our very baptism to be sent ones telling others about the one who has healed us of our blindness? Surely, we Christians who partake of the water of baptism, and eat the bread and drink the cup of the Lord's Supper, know the assistance which has come to our faith through such physical elements.

The other idea here is that Jesus got his hands dirty and defiled himself by dealing in such a manner with the man. Are there not times when we too must get ourselves dirty and defiled if our evangelism is to be effective?

Variety of Responses

Look with me now at the variety of responses to the man's healing. First, see how the neighbors responded. "Is not this the man who used to sit and beg?" (v. 8), the neighbors asked. "Some said, 'It is he'; others said, 'No, but he is like him' " (v. 9). Such curiosity, how very revealing. One wonders if these neighbors had ever really and truly looked at the man.

Second, see how the Pharisees responded to his healing (see vv. 13-17). Their problem was that the man had been healed on the sabbath. That meant that he was healed by a lawbreaker, and thus a sinner! Surely no such sinner could open eyes blind from birth. If God were going to do a thing like that, he would certainly not use a sabbath breaker to do it, they must have reasoned.

Third, see the response of a man's parents (vv. 18-23). They were so afraid of being excommunicated from the synagogue that they answered: "We know that this is our son, and that he was born blind; but how he now sees we do not know, nor do we know who opened his eyes. Ask him; he is of age, he will speak for himself" (vv. 20-21).

Fourth, see the response of the man to his own healing. To the neighbors he said, "I am the man" (v. 9). To the Pharisees he said, "He put clay on my eyes, and I washed, and I see" (v. 15). To his parents, the man evidently said nothing lest he place them further in danger of excommunication.

Then, the healed man rises to a great height when he says, "One thing I know, that though I was blind, now I see" (v. 25). Is that not the quintessence of a personal testimony? We may not be able to answer all of the questions put to us. We may not be able to articulate answers to the theological problems which our healing presents. But if God has opened our blind eyes, we can always testify, "One thing I know, that though I was blind, now I see."

Progression in Understanding

We may also see the progression in the man's understanding of who Jesus was. John 9:11 indicates that about all he knew about his healer was that he was "the man called Jesus." Then, in verse 17 the man confessed to the Pharisees, "He is a prophet." Third, in verse 33, the man clearly confesses that this man was from God because he had performed such a stupendous miracle.

The fourth and final movement in the man's progressive understanding of who Jesus was may be seen in verses 35-38. Jesus found him after he had been excommunicated from the synagogue and said, "Do you believe in the Son of man?" (v. 35). The man answered, "And who is he, sir, that I may believe in him?" (v. 36). Jesus said to him, "You have seen him, and it is he who speaks to you" (v. 37). Therefore, the man's faith is climaxed, "Lord, I believe" (v. 38).

This man was not instantly healed by Jesus. He was healed only when he washed in the pool of Siloam. Nor did he instantly believe in Jesus as the Son of man and worship him. That too came slowly and progressively. Is this not a model to teach us that not every person is instantly made completely whole by Jesus? Some persons have to have time for their faith to grow and mature. And isn't it an occasion for thanksgiving that Jesus meets us at our specific points of need and does not refuse to welcome us even when we come on such halting terms?

The Mystery of Suffering

A final point raised by this case is that suffering surrounds evangelism with a mystery. That mystery is pointed to in the question raised by the disciples of Jesus, "Rabbi, who sinned, this man or his parents, that he was born blind?" (v. 2). Again, we see it raised in the bitter retort of the Pharisees, "You were born in utter sin, and would you teach us?" (v. 34).

Jesus emphatically did not attribute all suffering to sin, either one's own or his parent's. His novel answer is "that the works of God might be made manifest in him" (v. 3).

Yet in spite of that innovative answer by the world's greatest authority, we still know that there is mystery in the meaning of suffering. Perhaps our best clue to the meaning of that mystery may be seen in the sufferings of Christ.

Isaiah presents to us a picture of the suffering servant:

> Surely he has borne our griefs
>   and carried our sorrows;
> yet we esteemed him stricken,
>   smitten by God, and afflicted.
> But he was wounded for our transgressions,
>   he was bruised for our iniquities;
> upon him was the chastisement that
>   made us whole,
>   and with his stripes we are healed.
> All we like sheep have gone astray;
>   we have turned every one to his own way;
> and the Lord has laid on him
>   the iniquity of us all (53:4-6).

9

One Who Had Been Dead Four Days

Daniel 12:2-3; John 11:1-53

This is the miracle of miracles in John's Gospel, the sign of all signs. I believe there are seven miracles listed in the Gospel of John. This is number seven—the symbolical number of perfection.

There can be no question about whether the case relates to evangelism. John 11:4 tells us: "This illness is not unto death; it is for the glory of God, so that the Son of God may be glorified by means of it." Then, note the confession of Martha in verse 27: "Yes, Lord; I believe that you are the Christ, the Son of God, he who is coming into the world." Also, Jesus' prayer "on account of the people standing by, that they may believe that thou didst send me" (v. 42) shows the relationship of this sign to evangelism.

Moreover, following the raising of Lazarus, we are told in verse 45: "Many of the Jews therefore, who had come with Mary and had seen what he did, believed in him." Even the chief priests and Pharisees said in verse 48: "If we let him go on thus, every one will believe in him."

One very unusual thing about the case is that Lazarus may well have already been a believer in Jesus. It appears that he was a saved man whose death and resurrection were used to evangelize unbelievers!

Life Out of Death

Jesus brings life out of death. Three times in the Gospels Jesus deals with death. Once, he deals with the daughter of Jairus (see Mark 5:21-24,35-43) who had just died. He raised her from her deathbed. Again, he raised the son of the widow of Nain from his coffin (see Luke

7:11-17). The funeral was in progress, and he broke it up. Now, in John 11 Jesus raises a man from the dead, one who was already in the tomb! Finally, Jesus dealt with death in his own death and resurrection. Perhaps the progressive difficulty of the cases is accidental. Nevertheless, the arrangement is instructive.

Jesus is in the business of raising the dead, both those who are dead physically and those who are dead in trespasses and in sins. C. H. Spurgeon has a soul-winning sermon on "How to Raise the Dead." It is a sermon on child evangelism. Evangelism is raising the dead! It is bringing life out of death.

Hear the mighty Son of God who was raised from the dead: "I am the resurrection and the life; he who believes in me, though he die, yet shall he live, and whoever lives and believes in me shall never die. Do you believe this?" (vv. 25-26).

Just as God created the world out of nothing, so, through Jesus Christ he creates life where there is death. The new creation is after the analogy of the old and first creation of Genesis 1. Evangelism is bringing order out of chaos. Evangelism is separating the light from darkness, and causing the light to rule over the darkness. Evangelism is bringing life where there is death.

Death Not the End

A second evangelistic truth to note in the case of Lazarus is that death is certainly not the end of existence. This case introduces us to another of the great "I am" sayings of Jesus. "I am the bread of life," Jesus said (John 6:35). And, so he is heaven's bread for mankind's hunger. By implication he is also the water of life (see John 4:14 and 7:37). "I am the light of the world" (John 8:12). Now he who is the bread of life, the water of life, and the light of life, tells us: "I am the resurrection and the life" (v. 25).

Physical death does not end existence. This is an important truth for both Christians and lost persons. Believers are comforted to know that there is a life beyond this life. Both believers and unbelievers need to know that death cannot end their existence. If one thinks he or she can end it all by suicide, he or she is mistaken. We reap what we sow. There is no escape in this world or in the next.

John M. Templeton is a Presbyterian layman who sponsors an annual Prize for Progress in Religion, a sort of Nobel for spiritual creativity which carries a $220,000 stipend. "The astronomers," said Templeton, "have taught us that there are 100 billion other galaxies and that we are not more important than any of them—all of which teaches us how infinite God is and how temporary we are."[1] Templeton and our temporariness in this present life notwithstanding, the case of one who had been dead four days teaches us that physical death is not the end of human beings.

A Place for Tears

There is a place for tears in evangelism. "Jesus wept" (v. 35). That may be the shortest verse in the Bible. L. R. Scarborough ventures the opinion that the tears of Jesus were his secret in winning persons.[2]

Luke 19:41 tells us that Jesus wept over Jerusalem. So, he who wept over the grave of his friend also wept over an unrepentant city. The writer of Hebrews also refers to the tears of Jesus: "In the days of his flesh, Jesus offered up prayers and supplications, with loud cries and tears, to him who was able to save him from death, and he was heard for his godly fear" (5:7).

Furthermore, we have a fitting word from the psalmist which teaches us that the weepers win: "May those who sow in tears reap with shouts of joy! He that goes forth weeping, bearing the seed for sowing, shall come home with shouts of joy, bringing his sheaves with him" (126: 5-6).

There is a sense in which seminaries were begun to help ministers of the gospel weep over the lost. Protestant seminaries in America began during the nineteenth century. President Donald W. Shriver, Jr., of Union Theological Seminary in New York, has said:

Look over the evolution of the seminary as an institution of 19th century American church history, and you will find that the founders so valued the church and its mission in this emerging frontier country, that they yearned for an education for church leadership more powerfully focused on that mission than the colleges of the land were accomplishing. They affirmed the colleges, but experience taught them that Charles G. Finney was right in describing some young ministers as coming "out of college with hearts as hard as the college walls." The evangelical revivals, the Second Great Awakening, explains the invention of the seminary.[3]

Have you wept over the dead lately? I don't mean merely over those who have died in the Lord. Have you wept over those who have died without hope? Have you wept over those loved ones and friends who are dead in trespasses and in sins? When we stop weeping, we may also stop winning. Let us ask God for the compassion and the capacity to weep over sin which leads ultimately to the second death and to eternal separation from God. Those among us who have difficulty weeping over the lost might well beseech God to open up our tear ducts.

Tenderness of Heart

Death often brings a tenderness of heart. I urge that we guard against "buzzard evangelism" with all our might. We Christians do not sit around like vultures and wait until someone dies to evangelize. God forbid! On the other hand, we must be wise enough to recognize that when death invades our ranks, it often brings a tenderness of heart which may prepare the broken-hearted to be touched with the tender, healing hand of the Lord.

No one can heal a broken heart like Jesus, the one who wept over the grave of his friend Lazarus. How sensitive we ought to be when the angel of death, that great leveler, visits any of our lost loved ones or friends or neighbors or acquaintances. One's family and friends who experience the loss of a loved one to death are at that moment and immediately thereafter most open to the change of conversion.

Interestingly enough, what has been said about the death of a loved one also is true of the death of a nation or of the death of a prized dream.

On one occasion I had the privilege of hearing Commander Mitsuo Fuchida on a radio program. Fuchida led the Japanese air attack on Pearl Harbor. Following the war, Fuchida heard that Americans had been torturing their Japanese prisoners. That made him even more bitter against the Americans for dropping the atom bomb on Hiroshima and Nagasaki.

While searching for evidence to confirm the atrocities of Americans against the Japanese, Fuchida talked with a friend who had been imprisoned in Utah. The friend told Fuchida about a nurse whose parents were missionaries and had been murdered by the Japanese in the Philippines. Yet, she had nursed injured Japanese soldiers back to health with love and kindness.

That story deeply moved Fuchida. While he was still shaken up, a tract was given him which told about an American bombardier who had been captured and tortured by the Japanese in a prison camp. One day a Japanese guard gave the bombardier a Bible. The American, who violently hated his captors, read in that Bible about Christ's love and redemption. When he believed in Christ, his hate was changed to love.

About that same time a Japanese translation of the Bible fell into Fuchida's hands. In Luke 23 he read about Christ's prayer just before he died. "I met Jesus that day," Fuchida said. "He came into my heart and changed my life from a military officer to a warrior for Christ." Fuchida turned down the highest position in the Japanese air force so he could preach the gospel of the kingdom of God.[4]

The Fourth Day Concept

John 11:17 says Lazarus had been in the tomb four days. There is a rabbinical tradition which said the soul hovers by the grave three days in hopes of reunion with the body, but at the first sign of decomposition, it departs finally. Conceivably, some great one might be able to raise the dead during the first three days, but only the greatest power could raise the body after it had begun to decompose!

Jesus is in the business of raising the dead—those who are dead in trespasses and in sins. Even the soul which has begun to rot and decompose because of sin can be made whole and new again by the power of Jesus Christ, the strong Son of God.

Peter Wagner originated the term "the Fourth World" to describe the world of the lost—the world's three billion lost persons.[5] I should like to suggest another term to accompany that of the Fourth World, namely the fourth day. We have a "fourth day" gospel for the Fourth World! Hallelujah! What a Savior!

Does your evangelism make allowances for a Savior who can raise a man from the dead even after he had been dead four days or longer? Does your gospel have a fourth day dimension in it? R. G. Lee used to say that if Jesus had not called the name of Lazarus, all the dead of all the centuries would have come forth when Jesus said: "Lazarus, come out" (v. 43). I submit to you that is a fourth day gospel.

One of the most precious promises which we may claim is found in the prophet Joel: "I will restore to you the years which the swarming locust has eaten" (Joel 2:25). By the way, this promise is in the same chapter of Joel from which Peter quotes in his sermon on the day of Pentecost.

How much do you know about locusts, or just plain grasshoppers? A pioneer woman in Kansas remembered grasshoppers in 1874 stripping not only the crops but also clothes from the settlers' backs. "They looked like a great, white glistening cloud, for their wings caught the sunshine on them and made them look like a cloud of white vapor."[6]

I can tell you that a fourth day gospel is required to restore to any one the years which the locust has eaten. Some of us, God forgive us, spent years of our lives which the swarming locusts of this world ate and devoured. They were years of waste and worry, years of prodigality and pride, years of shame and slavery to the weak and beggarly powers of this passing age. But, because our gospel is a fourth-day gospel, like Gabriel Heater, we have good news to share from the battlefront: "I will restore to you the years which the swarming locust has eaten."

Only a powerful fourth day gospel will suffice against the principalities and powers which now array themselves against God and against legitimate governments. The Nationalist Fascia of Europe had as its motto in 1980: "One God alone: Adolf Hitler." Another group, the Military Sports Group Hoffman has the motto: "We need a dictator—Fatherland, we are coming." Racism and fascism and Nazism are not dead. They are alive and well, as the resurgent Ku Klux Klan in America will attest.

Eternal Life as a Present Possession

Eternal life may be seen in this case as a present possession for those who believe. It is not just something hoped for in the future, following physical death. That is at least a part of the meaning of John 11:25-26. Martha's faith was in the Jesus of four-days ago, and in the Jesus who would raise the dead "in the resurrection at the last day" (v. 24). She, at that moment, did not believe in the Jesus of today.

I do not say that to be critical of Martha. We are like her. We believe more easily in the Jesus of the past and in the Jesus of the future than we do in the Jesus of the present. Sure Jesus did mighty deeds in the first century during the days of his flesh. Certainly he will work great wonders when he returns in power to consummate our salvation. Our faith needs to do some growing in the present. That same Jesus of the past and of the future is our Savior today. Eternal life is not relegated to the future following the second coming and death and the judgment. Right now and right here in the midst of time and space we are experiencing eternal life.

Jesus is not a fabled character like Beowolf. Bethlehem is not a fabled city like Camelot. Bus number 42 runs every thirty minutes from Bethany to Jerusalem. The whole drama of Christianity is acted out in real places by historical characters.

Life is not just a succession of dreary days, weeks, months, and years. Don't just fill your life with years, fill your years with life. Eternal life is Life with a capital L in the here-and-now as well as in the there-and-then.

The Role of Thomas

The case of Lazarus shows us the role of a Thomas in evangelism. "Thomas, called the Twin, said to his fellow disciples, 'Let us also go, that we may die with him'" (v. 16). Thomas has a position of prominence in the Gospels. The doubter is always present, even among the disciples. Thomas was a type of the original man from Missouri, the "show me" state.

"The greatest difficulty in the way of evangelism," wrote Professor L. R. Scarborough, "is the doubts of God's people. The block of unfaith kept Jesus from doing mighty works in Nazareth and in a thousand places since."[7] We can be sure that there is a Thomas in almost every congregation. Occasionally a church will be blessed (or plagued) with a whole family or a complete tribe of Thomases.

Have you encountered a Thomas in your evangelism, albeit under

some other name? If not, you will. More apropos still, are you yourself a
Thomas? It's all right to be a Thomas, provided you come to the point
the real Thomas did when he confessed the risen Christ to be "My Lord
and my God!" (John 20:28).

Notes

1. Quoted by *Newsweek,* March 9, 1981, p. 72.

2. See Scarborough, *How Jesus Won Men,* pp. 263-67.

3. Donald W. Shriver, Jr., "The Accountability of Theological Education to
the Mission of the Church," *Theological Education,* Vol. XVII, No. 1, Autumn,
1980, p. 60.

4. The story is also related by Chevis F. Horne, in "How to Create Surprise in
the Pulpit," *The Baptist Program,* February, 1981, p. 11.

5. See my *Church Growth—A Mighty River* (Nashville: Broadman Press,
1981), pp. 55-56.

6. Quoted by *Newsweek,* March 16, 1981, p. 88, in Peter S. Prescott's
review of *Pioneer Women: Voices From the Kansas Frontier,* by Joanna L.
Stratton (Simon and Schuster).

7. Scarborough, *How Jesus Won Men,* p. 137.

10

The Rich Young Ruler

Exodus 20:1-17; Mark 10:17-22

New Testament parallels to Mark 10:17-22 are Matthew 19:16-22 and Luke 18:18-30. We call this the case of the rich young ruler. All the parallels say he was rich. Matthew says he was a "young man" (Matt. 19:20). Luke 18:18 calls him "a ruler." Therefore, he was a rich young ruler.

Furthermore, we learn from the Scriptures that this rich young ruler was a man of high morals, a seeker after eternal life, and one who believed Jesus to be a good teacher. He even took the initiative in coming to Jesus, as did Nicodemus.

Negative Decisions

Decisions in evangelism may be negative as well as positive. This man's score was perfect on the negatives of religion. He had obeyed all of the "Do Nots." For example, Jesus said to him, "You know the commandments: 'Do not kill, Do not commit adultery, Do not steal, Do not bear false witness, Do not defraud . . . '" (v. 19). The rich young ruler said, "Teacher, all these I have observed from my youth" (v. 20).

Persons do have a right to make negative decisions. They are free and responsible individuals. The rich young ruler exercised his right to say no to eternal life.

This is not the only time Jesus struck out. He struck out in his own hometown of Nazareth (see Matt. 13:53-58). Matthew 13:58 says, "And he did not do many mighty works there, because of their unbelief." Jesus also struck out with the Gerasenes. Mark 5:17 says of the

Gerasenes, "And they began to beg Jesus to depart from their neighborhood."

Let us face this fact of evangelism squarely and candidly. Some persons are offended by Jesus. Some will choose not to welcome his intrusion into their lives. Some will say no to him and to his offer of eternal life. The rich young ruler did. His hometown folk of Nazareth did. The Gerasenes did.

You and I in our evangelizing can expect some negative decisions too. The servant is never greater than his or her master. Such negative decisions are after all a part of humanity's dignity. God has so created persons, and crowned them with such glory and honor, that they can say no to their Creator, Sustainer, and Redeemer.

Measurement of Success

Success in evangelism may not be measured entirely by the number of persons who says yes to Jesus Christ. Rather, being faithful to the gospel and to our opportunities to share it is success by God's standards. We are not at liberty to change the message. We dare not water down the gospel in order to secure positive decisions.

Jesus did not tone down his message for the sake of adding a promising young man to the kingdom. Jesus offered no false pretenses, no basement bargains. He did not conceal the cross or disguise the cost of discipleship. "Christ 'lost his man,' " as Halford E. Luccock says, "but he did not lose his gospel. And what shall it profit a church if it gain all the rich people in the world, and lose its own message?"[1]

I have from time to time requested my students to write up a personal witnessing experience which did not result in the respondent's salvation. I believe there is much to be learned from such cases. One such case which a student wrote up told of his "first honest attempt to tell someone the Good News with his ultimate conversion in mind." The prospect was a man to whom the student witnessed over a three-day period. "Perhaps a major block in this man's life that prevented him from letting go, was his material wealth," wrote the student. "He was ambitious and worked hard to the point that he owned 13 or 15 houses. I suspect this was his major problem. He was a self-made man and saw no need of a personal God in his life."[2]

Another point which struck me in that case was that the student said he tried to tell the prospect "that God wasn't a God of don'ts, but a God of do's."[3] Perhaps we do need to learn to measure our success in evangelism more by faithfulness to our opportunities and to our gospel than by whether the prospect says yes to Jesus Christ. And even if the answer is no, we can still learn from the encounter.

False Understanding of Salvation

Some would-be disciples have a false understanding of salvation. There are those who think salvation is a matter of good deeds. Such may have been the case with this man.

The question, "Good Teacher, what must I do to inherit eternal life?" (v. 17), reveals at least three things. First, the rich young ruler believed Jesus was a "Good Teacher." His perception of Jesus was that of a good teacher, and not necessarily that of a prophet or of the Savior of the world. Second, the questioner seemed to conceive of eternal life as something he must *do* in order to inherit it. Is eternal life something one earns through good works? The question points in that direction. Third, the man evidently believed that if he met certain conditions, he could *inherit* eternal life. Perhaps he had inherited his wealth and felt that if he met the right conditions he could inherit eternal life as well. The fact that he was a young man and already very wealthy lends some credence to that supposition.

But, alas! To be saved, a person has to see Jesus as more than a good teacher. He must be seen as Lord and Savior. Furthermore, we are saved by grace through faith. This is not our own doing. It is the gift of God, and not the result of our own good works, lest we boast of our own goodness. We are in fact God's workmanship, God's work of art, "created in Christ Jesus for good works, which God prepared beforehand, that we should walk in them" (see Eph. 2:8-10).

The Ethical Dimension

Moral values cannot be reduced to cash values or to sensory experience. It will cost us something to follow Christ. It will cost us our very life! Those who would follow Christ will have to jettison the false god of mammon. That idol of gold which one worships will have to be dethroned.

The same person who gave us the Great Commission (see Matt. 28:16-20) also gave us the great commandment (see Matt. 22:34-40). In fact, the Matthean form of this case includes the words, "You shall love your neighbor as yourself" (Matt. 19:19). So, alongside the other commandments, the author sets this second half of the twin-love commandment from Matthew 22.

Evangelism and ethics ought to be good friends. They ought to keep close company with one another. This case of the rich young ruler shows the interfacing of ethics and evangelism.

The Socratic Element

Socrates was a master at asking questions which generated substantive answers. So was Jesus. See, therefore, in this case the Socratic element in evangelism. Jesus answered the man's question with a question of his own, "Why do you call me good? No one is good but God alone" (v. 18).

See how one question may lead to another question in evangelism. Jesus is a master at Socratic evangelism. We also saw that in the case of Nicodemus in John 3.

There is, in fact, some similarity between the case of the rich young ruler and the case of Nicodemus. Both were rulers. Both came inquiring of Jesus about eternal life. Both took the initiative in seeking out Jesus. Both believed Jesus to be an unusual teacher. Both were full of questions. Both cases have to do with entrance into the kingdom of God. The Lucan parallel, along with Mark, actually incorporates the phrase, "kingdom of God" (see Luke 18:18-25), whereas the Matthean parallel uses both phrases, "kingdom of heaven" and "kingdom of God" (see Matt. 19:23-24).

But, back to the question Jesus put to the rich young ruler. Note that Jesus answered his own question, "No one is good but God alone" (v. 18). Does Jesus wish the young man to connect him with God? My guess is that he does indeed. Those who go around calling Jesus

"Good" anything should reflect upon the implication of that adjective.

Building Upon What Is There

We should in our evangelism build upon whatever foundation of truth or of goodness there is in the inquirer. Jesus did. All truth is God's truth and all moral goodness is ultimately derived from God, who is alone good.

Six of the ten commandments are specified in verse 19. Matthew throws in the new love commandment, "You shall love your neighbor as yourself" (Matt. 19:19). To them all, the rich young ruler consciously says, "Teacher, all these I have observed from my youth" (v. 20). Jesus is dealing here with one who knows the Decalogue, and who seeks to order his life by its legal requirements.

Note that Jesus does not contradict the rich young ruler's claim. On the contrary. Mark says, "And Jesus looking upon him loved him, and said to him, 'You lack one thing . . . ' " (v. 21). See how Jesus built upon what was there. Jesus affirmed the man and complimented him insofar as he had progressed and obeyed.

You and I very much need to learn to affirm our prospects in that which is already right in their lives. We need to recognize that our task is not to tear down anything which is good or truthful or beautiful which is already present in their lives. Indeed, that very truth may become our beginning point with them. We may build from that the remainder of the life foundation which is missing. Even when we are dealing with people of other religious persuasions, we can begin to build upon whatever foundation of truth and light they may have.

Some persons are not as far away from the kingdom as others. Those who are waiting just outside the door may only need someone to show them the way, and to invite them to come inside. Others who are prodigals, living in some faraway land of darkness and degradation, may need more illumination and more love before they will become citizens of heaven.

It is instructive for us to see how Paul built upon what was already there in his message on Mars' Hill (Acts 17:16-34). He quoted one of their inscriptions (Acts 17:23) and also the words of Epimenides and Aratus (Acts 17:28).[4]

Love for All Sinners

Jesus loves all sinners, and especially those sinners who are lost. Please look again at verse 21, "And Jesus looking upon him loved him." Therefore, John 3:16 is by no means the only Scripture which tells us about the love of God for sinners.

I think that love must have shown in the countenance and manner of Jesus toward the rich young ruler. I say that because of the contrast between Mark 10:21 and Mark 10:22. Mark seems to pick up on the body language of both Jesus and the ruler. The very countenance of Jesus must have lighted up with love as he beheld the young man. But when the cost was set forth, the countenance of the ruler "fell."

United Methodist Bishop Roy Nichols has shared a modern parable about a young woman who went to see her psychiatrist. She was a wife and the mother of three children. Almost at random the doctor asked, "Which of your three children do you love the most?" Instantly, the woman answered, "I love all three of my children the same."

The psychiatrist paused, thinking her answer was too quick and too glib. He decided to probe a bit further. "Come, now, you love all three of your children the same?" "Yes, that's right, I love all of them the same," she said. "Come off it now!" said the doctor. "It is psychologically impossible for anyone to regard any three human beings exactly the same. If you are not willing to level with me, we'll have to terminate this session."

With that the young woman broke down, cried some, and said, "All right, I do not love all three of my children the same. When one of the three is sick, I love that child more. When one of my children is confused, I love that child more. When one of them is in pain, or lost, I love that one more. And when one of my children is bad—I don't mean naughty, I mean really bad—I love that child more." Then, the lady added, "But except for these exceptions I do love all three of my children about the same."

Bishop Nichols, through this modern parable, is trying to say that God knows and loves you just as he loves all other persons on this planet. There is, however, according to the bishop, one addition: namely, when you are sick or hurting or lost or confused or in pain or depraved, God loves you even more. That's the reason we personalize the message of God's love as Augustine did when he said, "God loves each one of us as if there were only one of us to love."[5]

A good many years ago I had preached a sermon on the love of God one Sunday night to a congregation in Richmond, Virginia. Following the service, I went to the vestibule to greet the people. I was filling in for a pastor who was away conducting a revival meeting. Out of the corner of my eye, I noticed an eleven- or twelve-year-old boy who kept waiting around at a distance until everybody else was gone. Then, he came over to me, shook my hand and said, "Preacher, I want to ask you a question."

I braced myself, because I had learned that boys like that can ask hard questions. He said, "Who does God love most, saints or sinners?" My honest answer at the time was, "I really don't know who God loves most, saints or sinners." But that question has never left me. Since then, I have come to feel that while God loves us all with an everlasting love, he probably loves most that person who needs his love the most. Bishop Nichols' modern parable answers that lad's question to my satisfaction.

Lacking Just One Thing

Some would-be disciples are lacking just one thing in order to inherit eternal life. That one thing lacking for the rich young ruler was the proper disposal of his wealth (v. 21). That one thing lacking for the man who had been paralyzed for thirty-eight years was the desire to be healed (see John 5:6). That one thing lacking for those who would surrender everything but their intellect to Jesus Christ is to bring their intellect under captivity to Christ. That one thing lacking for others may be attachment to some appetite of the flesh such as sex or food or drugs.

Many may of course lack more than *one* thing in order to be saved. But clearly, this man lacked only one thing. He would not part with his possessions. Mammon was his master. "For the love of money is the root of all evils;" wrote the apostle Paul, "it is through this craving that some have wandered away from the faith and pierced their hearts with many pangs" (1 Tim. 6:10).

Jesus is the Great Physician. He does not prescribe the same pill for every patient. Probably, we should say that Jesus is the Great Surgeon General of the world. What Jesus prescribed for the rich young ruler was a radical surgical operation, "You lack one thing; go, sell what you have, and give to the poor, and you will have treasure in heaven; and come, follow me" (v. 21).

Let us learn to look for the one great thing which is missing in the persons with whom we deal. Then, let us, as did Jesus, boldly prescribe whatever surgery or medicine or cure may be necessary for them to inherit eternal life.

Contrast Between Beginning and Ending

We can see in this case the contrast between a sincere beginning and a sorrowful ending in evangelism. The rich young ruler came so eagerly. Mark says he "ran up and knelt before him" (v. 17). His coming even seemed urgent. Jesus "was setting out on his journey" (v. 17) and the ruler detained him. Yet, he left so sorrowfully with a fallen countenance and with a dejected demeanor (see v. 22). So many would-be followers of Jesus get a good start, but experience a sad finish.

I recall visiting a lost man in Tennessee in 1980 whom I shall call Jake. His father began as an evangelist and a singer. At that time Jake's father was divorced, an alcoholic, and no longer attended church, let alone practicing the ministry to which God called him. The father was living nearby but had never even seen his two-year-old grandson. It was difficult for me to witness to this lost mechanic because his own father had begun so well and ended so poorly.

During my nearly two decades of evangelistic ministry, I have seen not a few young ministers who aspired to be evangelists. They were so eager and willing. They began so promisingly. But, once they found out what it would cost them to be effective evangelists, most of them have gone away sadly and silently, not willing to pay the price.

I consider myself a kind of Barnabas to seminary students who aspire to a vocation in evangelism. One occupational hazard which seems to beset such seminarians is a temptation to take a shortcut in their formal education. They are tempted to drop out before they finish. So few vocational evangelists in the whole church are willing to pay the price of securing a first-rate theological education. Consequently, they begin well, but they experience early burnout or some other kind of shipwreck.

That reminds me of the story I heard a long time ago about the evangelist who strutted into the pulpit like a peacock with his feathers all spread out. He failed miserably and came down from the pulpit looking like a defeated dog with his tail dragging between his legs. Someone said as he beheld the spectacle, "If he had gone up into the pulpit like he came down from it, he would have come down like he went up!"

My advice in evangelism, as in all other aspects of the Christian life, is to start low, aim high, and then strike fire. We should aim not only for a good beginning but also for a good ending. Those who are willing to pay the price can turn a small beginning into a great and glorious ending.

Staircase of Verbs

I am struck by the *strong, ascending* staircase of verbs in our Lord's dealings with the rich young ruler. Look at those verbs in Mark 10:21: *lack, go, sell, give, come, follow.* They are put together like this, "You lack one thing; go, sell what you have, and give to the poor, and you will have treasure in heaven; and come, follow me" (v. 21).

Our Lord's prescription used strong verbs. He didn't pull any punches. These are active action verbs, not passive ones. There is a place for strong, active verbs in our witnessing. Moreover, there is a place for strong, vigorous, clear-cut actions in Christian discipleship. The response which our Lord seeks, demands and requires certain actions of all who would partake of life eternal.

Then, do not overlook the ascending staircase nature of the verbs our Lord used. He would have his disciples to realize their *lack; go,* or move out toward the property handlers of the world; *sell* that property or turn it into liquid assets; *give* that liquid capitol to the poor in order to open a bank account in heaven; and, *come* back and *follow* him wherever he leads. Hence, while the ruler only lacked one thing, the accomplishment of that thing involved an interconnected series of actions, each of which was a corollary of the other.

Spotting Discontent

Jesus quickly spotted the discontent which the rich young ruler had with his life. He was a straight-walking, straight-talking, splendid young man, but he was lost. He appeared on the surface to have everything together in his own life. There was a restlessness which drove him to Jesus.

Many are dissatisfied from drinking at the world's fountains. They are reaching out for something more. That "something more" is our opportunity to evangelize. So many moderns are question marks walking about in the flesh. Jesus is God's eternal yes to all the promises of God which may answer those questions (see 2 Cor. 1:20).

Notes

1. See Halford E. Luccock, "The Gospel According to St. Mark: Exposition," *The Interpreter's Bible,* Vol. VII (New York: Abingdon Press, 1951), p. 804.

2. This case was written up by Kenneth R. Gillespie in course 158, Contemporary Personal Evangelism, at Midwestern Baptist Theological Seminary, Kansas City, Mo., in March, 1981.

3. Ibid.

4. See F. F. Bruce, *Commentary on the Book of Acts* (Grand Rapids: Wm. B. Eerdmans, Publishing Co., 1955), pp. 359-60.

5. Related by George G. Hunter III, *The Contagious Congregation* (Nashville: Abingdon, 1979), pp. 74-75.

11

The Paralytic
Carried by Four Men

Psalm 103:1-5; Mark 2:1-12

We are looking today at the case of a paralytic carried by four men. The case is recorded for us in Mark 2:1-12. New Testament parallels to it are found in Matthew 9:1-8 and in Luke 5:17-26.

Psalm 103:3 lists two of God's benefits as follows, "who forgives all your iniquity, who heals all your diseases." The Bible does not, like so many of us, chop persons up into two parts labeled "soul" and "body," and confine God's salvation to man's soul. On the contrary, this ancient Hebrew poetry with its parallel lines is saying one thing in two different ways. Consequently, when the psalmist says, "who heals all your diseases," that is just another way of saying, "who forgives all your iniquity."

It was Greek philosophy and modern science which dichotomized man into body and mind, and trichotomized man into body, mind, and spirit (or soul). The Judeo-Christian view of man is much more wholistic. The biblical view of man is not nearly so chopped up as that. Incidentally, our tendency to substitute belief in the immortality of the soul for belief in the resurrection of the body also stems from this false "chopping up" of man.

The Place of the Home

The home is a good setting for evangelism. Mark 2:1 says in part, "It was reported that he was at home." We are not told whose home. Probably it was Peter's home. Most likely, it was not Jesus' home. According to Matthew's Gospel, Jesus had no home. "Foxes have holes, and birds of the air have nests; but the Son of man has nowhere to lay his head" (Matt. 8:20).

In many cultures the home is to this day the best place to evangelize. It offers privacy, comfort, and informality—all of which are assets to evangelizing. This is true whether we are meeting in a humble, rented apartment or in a spacious, private dwelling. Moreover, it is equally a good place whether we are meeting in our home or in the home of a prospect.

Michael Green has an excellent section on the value of home evangelism in his great work on *Evangelism in the Early Church*. Green says:

One of the most important methods of spreading the gospel in antiquity was by the use of homes. It had positive advantages; the comparatively small numbers involved made real interchange of views and informed discussion among the participants possible; there was no artificial isolation of a preacher from his hearers; there was no temptation for either the speaker or the heckler to "play to the gallery" as there was in a public place or open-air meeting. The sheer informality and relaxed atmosphere of the home, not to mention the hospitality which must often have gone with it, all helped to make this form of evangelism particularly successful.[1]

There are two aspects of home evangelism which we need to lift up. First, we should more readily use our own homes for evangelistic purposes. Christian hospitality in homes is rapidly becoming a lost art in many churches. God has given us nice homes and apartments that we might use them in his service.

How long has it been since you entertained lost persons in your home? How many new Christians have you entertained in your home? How long has it been since you invited strangers who visited your church on Sunday morning to break bread with you around your table? Have you considered volunteering your home for a Bible study in your community?

Second, we should take advantage of the golden opportunities which we still have in many places to visit lost persons in their homes. There are still many hundreds of thousands of homes and apartments where we can go even without an appointment. Other homes would be open to us by appointment. Some parts of America show a respect for God, the church, and the Bible which are great assets to home evangelism. We should take maximum advantage of these "open doors" while they are open.

I have related elsewhere how forty-four persons were led to Christ in their homes one Thursday night in about two hours.[2] I have seen more persons confess their faith in their home than in any other place. My experience teaches me that a person's home is his or her castle. That is where he or she is most in control. It is, therefore, one of the most appropriate places to share the gospel with unbelievers.

The Healthy Hindering the Sick

This case shows us that those who are healthy sometimes keep the sick from getting to Jesus. Those who are whole do not need the Great Physician as much as those who are sick.

Mark 2:2 says, "And many were gathered together, so that there was no longer room for them, not even about the door." Wherever Jesus is, he can gather a crowd. But sometimes that crowd prevents certain other individuals from coming to Jesus.

Doesn't Soren Kierkegaard somewhere speak of "the individual" over against "the masses," "the one" over against "the many"? If we may use those categories, "the many" sometimes hinders "the one" from coming to Christ; "the masses" sometimes prevents "the individual" or the few from getting into his saving presence.

Are you an obstacle, preventing others from coming to Jesus? Or, are you an opportunity for the really sick to come into our Lord's presence. To put it another way, are you a stumbling block or a stepping-stone? Do persons have to stumble over you in order to reach Jesus, or do you offer yourself as a stepping-stone on the path to the Master?

I get the feeling at times that we saved persons are so enamored with Jesus that we "hog" him for ourselves. We so crowd around him, and so long to sit at his feet, that often we don't leave any room for outsiders to get to him. Haven't you seen churches so concerned with feeding themselves on the Bread of life that they seem to forget about the hungry paralytics of the world who have been done in by the devil and sin?

When the "Christian crowd" gets in the way of the lost individuals, we see the healthy hindering the sick in evangelism. When we want so much of Jesus for ourselves that we make no room for others to get to him, our evangelism becomes half-baked. We become like Hosea's Ephraim, "a cake not turned" (Hos. 7:8).

Love Will Find a Way

Love will find a way to get our friends to Jesus. "And they came, bringing to him a paralytic carried by four men. And when they could not get near him because of the crowd, they removed the roof above him; and when they had made an opening, they let down the pallet on which the paralytic lay" (vv. 3-4).

They had to break up the roof. That's a creative way to "raise the roof" in evangelism. Love will find a way. Love will bear almost any burden. Love will go to great lengths to introduce one's friends to the Savior. Love will even break the rules in order to accomplish its mission. Again, evangelism is iconoclastic when it is inspired by Jesus. He broke a sabbath-day rule; these four friends broke the roof.

Creativity and innovation in our evangelistic methodology will come if we care enough for the paralytics of the world to bring them to Jesus. Love doesn't give up easily. Love will not be too quickly discouraged. Love always values persons above property.

When the four saw they could not get their friend to Jesus through the door, they resorted to plan B. Palestinian houses had flat roofs. These flat roofs were regularly used for rest and quiet relaxation. Usually they had an outside stair which ascended to them. The roof would consist of flat beams laid across from wall to wall, about three feet apart. The space between the beams was filled with brushwood and packed with clay. The roof was made mostly of earth. Sometimes a flourishing crop of grass grew on the roof. Hence, it would have been fairly easy for the four to dig out between two of the beams and let their friend down before Jesus. Not much damage would have been done to the roof. It could easily be repaired.[3] That was their plan B.

Have you ever "raised the roof" to bring a friend to Jesus? You may not know exactly how to bring your lost friends to Jesus. But, I can tell you this: love which is strong enough will find a way. It may not be so much the lack of proper methods as it is the lack of proper love, which prevents us from bringing our friends to Jesus.

Faith That Works Miracles

Our faith and faithfulness can work miracles in the lives of our lost friends and kinfolk. That is a fourth point made by this case of a paralytic carried by four men. Focus on Mark 2:5, "And when Jesus saw their faith, he said to the paralytic, 'My son, your sins are forgiven.'" Note the third person plural pronoun, "their." When he saw *their* faith, he pronounced forgiveness.

According to the four Gospels, Jesus marveled at the belief of certain Gentiles and at the unbelief of his own people. Matthew seems to indicate that the unbelief of his own fellow-townsmen limited the mighty works of Jesus in Nazareth (Matt. 13:58).

We know from Hebrews 3:19 that it was the unbelief of the Israelites which kept them from entering the Promised Land for forty years. They were sentenced to wander one year for every day the spies took to search out the land. Had they believed God, they could have gone in at once and possessed the land flowing with milk and honey. They had their eyes on the "giants" and on the high-walled cities rather than upon God.

Apparently there is some sense in which our unbelief limits the Eternal One, and some sense in which our faith liberates God to act on behalf of others as well as of ourselves. When Augustine's mother, Monica, went to Ambrose with her concern for her son's salvation, the man of God said something to this effect: "Go your way in peace; for it is impossible that the son of such tears should be lost." Shortly thereafter, Augustine was converted to Christ. Probably Susannah Wesley's faith and prayers had much to do with John Wesley's heartwarming experience on Aldersgate Street in London.

How many of us are somebody else's trophy of grace? How many of us owe our salvation, humanly speaking, to someone else's faith and labors which overcame every obstacle to lead us to Christ? How many of us now believe in Christ because some dear friend or loved one first believed in Christ, and in us? So, in a very real sense, *their* faith has brought us to Jesus Christ, the Faithful One who has numbered us with Abraham and with that whole company of men and women mentioned in Hebrews 11.

I like that epitaph on Lottie Moon's tombstone, "Faithful unto Death." If you and I will be faithful unto death, the fruit of such faith and faithfulness will surely be an evangelistic harvest that remains from among our lost loved ones and friends.

Unorthodox Methods

Jesus is not shocked when we use unorthodox methods to bring persons to him. Instead of rebuking the four who broke up the roof tiles, Jesus appears to have rewarded them. It was when he saw their faith that he pronounced forgiveness of sins to the paralytic (see v. 5).

When George Whitefield and John Wesley started preaching the gospel out-of-doors, the Anglican Church was shocked. Many preachers closed their pulpits to them. The church leaders were scandalized. Yet, it pleased God to raise up the Methodists and to bless the world through them. The singing of John and Charles Wesley was so different, and yet so divine. The Methodist class meetings and the circuit-riding system with its use of lay preachers was so shockingly different, and yet so marvelously blessed by God.

The Great Awakening in America was so different than previously used evangelistic methodology that it caused the church to split in many places along the two lines called "New Lights" and "Old Lights." That split continued when the frontier camp meetings began around the end of the eighteenth century. It was further accentuated in the first half of the nineteenth century when Charles G. Finney and Asahel Nettleton had their confrontation. Yet, it pleased God to raise up a new people out of that split called Separate Baptists.

These Separate Baptists who sided with the "New Lights" coming out of New England revivalism were the ones who started "The Sandy Creek Tradition" among Southern Baptists. It is from this tradition that Southern Baptists get their ardor which expresses itself in individualism, congregationalism, biblicism, and egalitarianism.[4]

The evangelistic methods which have made Southern Baptists the largest non-Roman Catholic denomination in America were at one time quite unorthodox. But it seems to please God to bless such unorthodox methods. Unorthodox evangelistic methods appear to upset some of God's "frozen" people more than they upset him. So long as our methods are ethical, and do not contradict our theology, we need not worry too much over them. The same God who gave our spiritual forebears appropriate evangelistic methods can be counted on today to give us the methods which we need.

Hard Cases

Jesus is not stymied or stopped when we bring our hard cases to him. He knew exactly how to deal with the paralytic who required four men to carry him. He knows what to do with all persons. No case is too hard for him. He can deal with what we may be prone to call "hopeless" cases.

Once again, I call your attention to the word of the Lord in Psalm 103:3-4, "Who forgives all your iniquity, who heals all your diseases, who redeems your life from the Pit." Jesus can deal with *all* iniquity, heal *all* diseases, and redeem one even from the Pit of Hades itself. His arm is not so shortened that it can't reach down to the lowest depth. His hand is not so weakened that it can't break up the most hardened heart.

Both the evangelist and the person being evangelized need to know that Jesus can save unto the uttermost all who come to him. He seems to delight in dealing with the most difficult cases. Jesus is the Great Physician who accepts even the cases on which all the others have given up. He specializes in treating the world's rejects and outcasts.

The Whole Person

The evangelism which pleases God is concerned with the whole person: body, mind, and soul. Jesus does not make the artificial distinction between the physical and the spiritual which we tend to make. He responds to whatever needs a person has. Physical healing does not necessarily imply spiritual healing. Nor does spiritual healing necessarily imply physical healing. But our health is important to God. One of the meanings of salvation is health and wholeness.

Jesus frequently dealt with the sick and infirmed. So often when persons are in physical distress and weak, they seem more aware of their limitations, and thus more open to God. As evangelists, we should be present whenever persons in physical and emotional distress need us.

Forgiveness of Sin

The heart of evangelism is the forgiveness of sin. Most of the case revolves around that. Actually Mark 2:5-12 treats the sin problem.

We Americans are apt to recoil at the mention of sin. After all, it was a psychiatrist, Karl Menninger, who raised the question *Whatever Became of Sin?* Menninger, writing in 1973, says, "As a nation, we officially ceased 'sinning' some twenty years ago." It was in 1953 when President Eisenhower stopped using the word *sin*. Menninger goes so far as to suggest that we might create a "no-fault" theology to deal with sin, much as we have created no-fault casualty insurance.

This book by the noted psychiatrist begins with an opening illustration which is worthy of our consideration in this context. It is a sunny day in September 1972. A stern-faced, plainly dressed man is standing on a street corner in the busy Chicago Loop. As pedestrians hurried on their way to lunch or business, he solemnly lifts up his right arm, points to the person nearest him, and loudly intones the single word *guilty!*

Over and over the man repeats the same process. Without changing his expression, he resumes his stiff stance for a few moments. Then, he raises his arm, points, and solemnly pronounces the one word *guilty!*

Can you imagine the effects of this strange pantomime on the passing strangers? They would stare at him, hesitate, look away, look at each other, and then at him again; then hurriedly continue on their ways.[5]

Of what were they guilty? Of many things, but most of all guilty of sin. You are guilty. I am guilty. We all are guilty of sin. As Paul said in Romans 3:23, "All have sinned and fall short of the glory of God." "None is righteous, no, not one" (Rom. 3:10).

But Jesus came into the world to save us from our sin, and to deal with that guilt. "My son, your sins are forgiven" (v. 5). Those words generated quite a discussion, "Why does this man speak thus? It is blasphemy! Who can forgive sins but God alone?" (v. 7). Who, indeed? Jesus spoke like that in order "that you may know that the Son of man has authority on earth to forgive sins" (v. 10).

Evangelism deals forthrightly with the problem of guilt created by sin.

Whatever else the evangelist may do, if he doesn't deal with guilt over sin and help persons find forgiveness for their sins, he is far from the mark. With all of our euphemisms for sin, and in spite of all of our own human remedies for sin, the problem of sin is still with us. And the only lasting answer to sin is forgiveness. "The blood of Jesus his Son cleanses us from all sin" (1 John 1:7).

Conclusion

This case of a paralytic carried by four men is a microcosm of the church and the world today. The world is filled with paralytics who need to be brought to Jesus. Some in the church are so "hogging" Jesus for themselves that they constitute a crowd of Christians through whom there is no room for outsiders to pass. Others in the church are like the four men. They are engaged in bringing the paralytics to Jesus in spite of the crowd and all other obstacles. Others in the church are like the scribes "sitting there, questioning in their hearts" (v. 6). They want to debate over which should come first, the salvation of the soul or the healing of the body.

Let us so work and hope and pray that when God heals a paralytic before our eyes, and when he forgives a sinner in our very midst, we shall be amazed and glorify God, saying, "We never saw anything like this!" (v. 12).

Notes

1. Michael Green, *Evangelism in the Early Church* (Grand Rapids: Wm. B. Eerdmans Publishing Co., 1970), pp. 207-208.

2. See my chapter, "An Example to Motivate Us," in *Evangelism Men: Motivating Laymen to Witness,* compiled by James A. Ponder (Nashville: Broadman Press, 1974), p. 97.

3. I am indebted to William Barclay for this description. See William Barclay, *The Gospel of Mark* (Philadelphia: The Westminster Press, 1956, 2nd ed.), pp. 39-40.

4. See Walter B. Shurden, "The Southern Baptist Synthesis: Is It Cracking?" Lecture I in The 1980-81 Carver-Barnes Lectures, Delivered at Southeastern Baptist Theological Seminary, Nov. 4-5, 1980, in *Outlook,* March-April, 1981, Vol. XXX, No. 5, p. 6.

5. See Karl Menninger, *Whatever Became of Sin?* (New York: Hawthorn Books, Inc., 1973), esp. pp. 1-2,14-15,188.

12

Zacchaeus

Exodus 22:1-4; Luke 19:1-10

We are looking now at the case of Zacchaeus as found in Luke 19:1-10. Some think this to be a variant of the story of Levi, the publican, in Luke 5:27-32 and in Mark 2:13-17. There are similarities in the stories, but also some important differences.

The word *Zacchaeus* means "pure" or "righteous." Does Dr. Luke have in mind the etymology of that word when he relates the story? Luke is aware of the incongruity of that name. Parents do not name their sons Nero or Judas, but Paul and Jude. The name Nero we reserve for our dogs.

The Rich Can Be Saved

Zacchaeus is an example of a rich person who was saved. Whereas the rich young ruler illustrated a rich person who refused to be saved (see Mark 10:22), Zacchaeus illustrates a rich person who wanted to be saved, and who was.

Jesus said to the rich young ruler, "How hard it is for those who have riches to enter the kingdom of God! For it is easier for a camel to go through the eye of a needle than for a rich man to enter the kingdom of God" (Luke 18:24-25). That prompted the disciples to ask, "Then who can be saved?" (Luke 18:26). Jesus said, "What is impossible with men is possible with God" (Luke 18:27). Hence, the case of Zacchaeus demonstrates that it is possible with God's help for a camel to pass through the eye of a needle!

Luke is the Gospel to the outcasts. Zacchaeus happened to be an outcast who was "up and out." He was an outcast because he was a tax collector. He was more of an outcast because "he was a chief tax collector, and rich" (v. 2).

No doubt, Zacchaeus was a very lonely man. Perhaps he was also an outcast because he was "small of stature." There may be a light touch of humor in Zacchaeus climbing up the sycamore tree. Even our society looks down on midgets! Those small of stature are frequently ignored and overlooked and slighted. That is in fact so much so that sometimes they themselves suffer from an inferiority complex.

Zacchaeus was not an outcast because he was rich. He was rich probably because he was a chief tax collector. His riches were probably ill gotten. He probably had sold his soul for "filthy lucre."

Let all who are rich in this world's goods take note. The rich can be saved. Zacchaeus is exhibit A.

Note also in this connection that Jesus related upward to Zacchaeus rather than downward. He loved rather than judged. We can see that especially in his dealings with Zacchaeus and with the woman taken in the very act of adultery.

Drawn Out of Curiosity

The text indicates that it was at first curiosity which drew Zacchaeus to Jesus, "And he sought to see who Jesus was, but could not, on account of the crowd, because he was small of stature. So he ran on ahead and climbed up into a sycamore tree to see him, for he was to pass that way" (vv. 3-4).

Zacchaeus may have been one of the first persons drawn to Jesus out of curiosity; he certainly was not the last one! Some persons in our day are drawn to him at first out of mere curiosity. They have heard about Jesus, but they have not heard him or seen him for themselves.

Jesus Takes Notice

Jesus notices those who notice him. Zacchaeus was richly rewarded for his efforts. Jesus was especially aware of outcasts. Zacchaeus may have been small of stature, but that didn't bother Jesus. If you happen to be small of stature, I have good news for you. Jesus loves you. Jesus is aware of you. Jesus sees you. Jesus will not overlook you.

Not all of us can be like the actor who stands only three feet and nine inches tall and confidently says: "Height does not mean anything. The only space barrier you . . . have to conquer is the one between your ears."[1]

Jesus never missed seeing anyone who wanted to see him. "Blessed are those who hunger and thirst for righteousness, for they shall be satisfied" (Matt. 5:6). The Scripture says, "Seek, and you will find; knock, and it will be opened to you. For every one who . . . seeks finds, and to him who knocks it will be opened" (Matt. 7:7-8).

Iconoclasm in Evangelism

Jesus was an iconoclast in his evangelism. He broke the sacred customs and traditions of his society in order to save persons. Instead of fitting the mold, Jesus broke it. He created his own molds, so to speak. The good folk were scandalized that Jesus would be the guest of a chief tax collector. They murmured: "He has gone in to be the guest of a man who is a sinner" (v. 7).

Persons are of infinitely greater worth to Jesus than the customs of polite society. He shattered the traditions of the elders to smithereens. Let the Christian disciple always value persons above pious platitudes. Let him or her feel good about doing what is right in the eyes of God, rather than doing what is expected in the eyes of a sensate culture.

The Initiative

Note that Jesus takes the initiative with Zacchaeus. "Zacchaeus, make haste and come down; for I must stay at your house today" (v. 5). We should learn how to take the initiative with the lost. We should meet them more than halfway. We should be second milers toward the unreconciled. We ought to at the very least be willing to meet them on their turf. Jesus did. This is the seeking element in evangelism.

That seems to be the significance of the statement in Luke 19:10, "For the Son of man came to seek and save the lost." Our God is a seeking Savior. He is like the faithful shepherd who seeks after the one lost sheep until he finds him. He is, as Francis Thompson says, the Hound of heaven who pursues us down all the labyrinthine ways of life.

John Bisagno spoke a fitting word when he told the 1981 Southern

Baptist Convention Pastors' Conference that pastors could never win the world to Christ "sitting behind a desk playing solitare with church prospect cards."[2] I believe we ought to seek after the lost as Jesus did.

If we are to pattern our evangelism after Jesus, we shall have to take the initiative with the Zacchaeuses who are up the sycamore trees of our world. One may think, "How forward of Jesus, inviting himself to the house of Zacchaeus! How audacious can you get?" But, remember, no self-respecting Jew had visited this chief tax collector since he had "sold" his soul to the Roman government. Jesus had far more in mind than a free meal. Bold measures are needed at times, especially when we are dealing with social outcasts.

Under New Management

Note the profound change which came about in Zacchaeus: "And Zacchaeus stood and said to the Lord, 'Behold, Lord, the half of my goods I give to the poor; and if I have defrauded any one of anything, I restore it fourfold' " (v. 8).

There ought to be some evidences in our converts that their lives are under new management. Have you ever noticed the sign on a business establishment, "Under New Management"? That sign ought to appear on every new Christian's life.

Zacchaeus made restitution beyond what the law required. Exodus 22:1 calls for a fourfold restitution when a sheep is stolen and a fivefold restitution when an ox is stolen. This converted tax collector gave half his goods to the poor, and offered a fourfold restitution to those whom he had defrauded.

T. B. Maston used the case of Zacchaeus to illustrate the close relation between evangelism and ethics. "They are," says Maston, "two sides of the same coin."[3]

Some of you may recall that underworld figure Jim Vaus was one of the big-name converts in Billy Graham's 1949 Los Angeles crusade. Vaus was the son of a prominent Los Angeles minister. He was thrown out of a Bible school, where he had gone to please his parents. Vaus drifted into a life of crime. By 1949 he was making big money as an electronics expert for that notorious Mickey Cohen, "Czar of the Los Angeles Underworld." He was also a key man for a gangster syndicate defrauding bookmakers by an ingenious system of split-second wiretapping which enabled their agents to place bets after a race had been won.

Following Vaus' conversion, under the preaching of thirty-year-old Billy Graham and the personal work of Uncle Billy Scholfield, the headlines read, "Wiretapper Vaus Hits Sawdust Trail."[4] I heard Jim Vaus a good many years after his conversion tell how difficult it was for him to make restitution for all the crimes and wrongs he had done. The fact that he did diligently seek to make restitution convinced me of the authenticity of his salvation.

We may not always make complete restitution immediately upon conversion. As I was discussing the case of Zaccheus with one of my classes, one of my students spoke up rather hesitatingly and said something like this: "Maybe I shouldn't share this, but when I was saved, I was working as a plumber. I found myself slipping wrenches into my tool box. Two years after my conversion I returned those big wrenches to the firm from which I had stolen them. Nobody knew it but I."

There is a word of Scripture from the apostle Paul which says, "If any one is in Christ, he is a new creation; the old has passed away, behold, the new has come" (2 Cor. 5:17). Those who are converted to Jesus Christ ought to give evidence that their lives are "Under New Management."

Evangelism On the Run

The case of Zaccheus is an example of evangelism on the run. There are four indications of this in the text. First, verse 1 says, "He entered Jericho and was passing through." Note those words "passing through." Second, verse 4 tells us of Zaccheus, "So he ran on ahead." Evidently Jesus was passing through rather quickly. It was necessary for Zaccheus to run in order to position himself in the path of Jesus. Third, in verse 5, Jesus said to the short publican, "Make haste and come down." Again, that points to the hurry of Jesus. Fourth, verse 6 says, "So he made haste and came down, and received him joyfully." Zaccheus didn't waste any time getting down out of that sycamore tree.

Jesus was in a hurry, but not in too much of a hurry to spend some time with Zacchaeus. The Gospel writers make it clear that Jesus was on his way to Jerusalem for his passion.

So much of the evangelism of Jesus was done while he was passing through, busy about some other appointment, intent on helping somebody else. When we feel rushed and harried and in such a hurry, we would do well to imitate the example of Jesus in our evangelism. It is possible to do evangelism "on the run." In fact, that may be a characteristic of so much of our evangelism today. Not only are we "on the run," but so are many of our prospects.

Jesus was a master at impromptu evangelism. He was prepared for the unexpected opportunity. Whenever an opportunity presented itself, he reached out and seized it. He may have been passing by, or passing through, but he never passed up an opportunity. What about you? Are you prepared to do evangelism on the run? Do you know how to latch on to the spontaneous possibilities?

Household Evangelism

The case of Zacchaeus is also probably another example of household, or *oikos* evangelism. The two significant references which use the Greek root, *oikos,* are verses 5 and 9. Both times it is Jesus who uses the word. Look: "I must stay at your house today," and "Today salvation has come to this house."

There is, to be sure, no explicit reference to other persons being saved besides Zacchaeus. However, the implication is that what happened to Zacchaeus happened to his whole household (see v. 9). Accordingly, this case is probably as much an example of *oikos* evangelism as is the case of the official whose son was ill (see John 4:46-54), and as are the cases of Cornelius (see Acts 10:1 to 11:18), Lydia (see Acts 16:14-15), and the Philippian jailor (Acts 16:19-34).

It is not stretching biblical truth to observe that when the head of a household is changed, his or her whole household is affected. The head of a house cannot be saved without his or her salvation having a blessing effect upon others who may be in that one's immediate realm of influence.

This is not intended to suggest that anyone can ever be saved apart from personal and individual faith in the Lord Jesus Christ. But, it is to say that while it is a blessed sight to see any person saved, it is even more blessed still to see the head of a household saved and to see other persons saved along with that key person. God still uses the webs of kinship and friendship and human association as the bridges across which he moves into the lives of our loved ones and friends and business associates.

Had we not all rather hear our Master say, "Today salvation has come to this house," than to merely hear him say, "Today salvation has come to you"? I believe the heretical practice of baptizing proxies for one's dead relatives may arise out of such concern for the salvation of one's household. But baptism of proxies for the dead notwithstanding, it is certainly more fun and provides more peace of mind and heart when we see our loved ones and dear friends saved along with us.

Mixed Response

A final point which the case lifts up for our edification is the mixed responses to Jesus. See how Zaccheus responded. He "received him joyfully" (v. 6). Then, see how others responded, "And when they saw it they all murmured, 'He has gone in to be the guest of a man who is a sinner' " (v. 7).

If there is any validity at all to seeing Luke 5:27-32 and Mark 2:13-17 as a variant to the case of Zaccheus, we may be helped at this junction to observe that Luke 5:31 and Mark 2:17 may give us a clue to understand better these two responses. Those who, like Zaccheus, receive Jesus joyfully are the "sick." On the other hand, those who, like the onlookers, murmur and make nasty remarks about Zaccheus and Jesus are the "well."

I sense a certain irony in the words of Jesus, "Those who are well have no need of a physician, but those who are sick; I have not come to call the righteous, but sinners to repentance" (Luke 5:31-32). Alas! Some are sick and don't know their true spiritual condition. They think they are well and have no need of a physician.

Woe to all such "well" souls. But blessed be such "sick," who know themselves to be lost and undone without God and without hope in this world or in the next. The Son of man met with a mixed reception in the first century, and in every succeeding century. To this very day some receive him joyfully, while others murmur and complain, "He has gone in to be the guest of a man who is a sinner."

Conclusion

I tell you, my friends, Jesus was *the* Friend of sinners. He is passing your way again today. If you want to see him, you had better make haste. Don't you hear him calling your name and inviting himself to eat with you today? I beseech you to receive him joyfully.

"Scriptures represent God as a seeking God," wrote A. C. Archibald. " 'Behold, I stand at the door and knock.' Our God is a God who has come down. He seeks for man."[5]

How thankful I am that one day Jesus walked right into my life. He invited himself to eat at my house. I gladly and gratefully welcomed him. Ever since that wonderful day, Jesus has been the unseen guest at every meal in my home. One day I expect him to invite me to go and live with him forever in his Father's house, where there are many rooms (see John 14:2-3).

Warner Sallman's famous picture of Christ knocking at the door of the heart comes to my mind.[6] The latch to that door is on the inside. "Behold, I stand at the door and knock; if any one hears my voice and opens the door, I will come in to him and eat with him, and he with me" (Rev. 3:20).

Notes

1. See the AP story, "Actor Doesn't Have to Reach for His Star," *The Kansas City Times,* July 3, 1981, p. A-2.

2. Quoted by *The Baptist Courier,* June 18, 1981, Vol. 113, No. 25, p. 4.

3. T. B. Maston, "Both/And: Evangelism and Ethics," *The Baptist Messenger,* Feb. 19, 1981, p. 12.

4. See John Pollock, *Billy Graham: The Authorized Biography* (New York: McGraw-Hill Book Co., 1966), pp. 59-61,63.

5. Arthur C. Archibald, *New Testament Evangelism* (Philadelphia: The Judson Press, 1946), p. 20.

6. For the creative use of Sallman's picture, see Charles "Chic" Shaver, *Conserve the Converts* (Kansas City, MO: Beacon Hill Press of Kansas City, 1976), pp. 21-22,81.

13

A Canaanite Woman

Isaiah 45:9-11; Matthew 15:21-28

We are now about to consider what L. R. Scarborough calls "one of the most remarkable stories in all the history of Christianity."[1] I refer to the case of a Canaanite woman in Matthew 15:21-28. Mark 7:24-30 presents a New Testament parallel to the case.

Withdrawal

Matthew begins his account of the case this way: "And Jesus went away from there and withdrew to the district of Tyre and Sidon" (v. 21). Withdrawal and retreat are sometimes necessary for effective evangelism. We can stay so long with the needy multitudes and the hungry crowds that we deplete our resources.

Even Jesus thought it necessary to withdraw at times. If Jesus, the perfect model man and the Son of God, felt the need to retreat, how much more should we?

One of the most profitable six weeks of my life was spent at the School of Pastoral Care in Winston-Salem, North Carolina, studying under the late Chaplain Richard K. Young. I recall how Chaplain Young told us that during the first few years of his ministry in Winston-Salem he gave himself with such abandonment to the patients that he went for a long period without taking any time off. Then, one day Young said, "I was so tired and weary that I said to myself, 'Even if you all die and go to hell, I'll just have to take some time off.'"

Chaplain Young was not abandoning the patients. He was simply withdrawing for a time of rest and restoration. He was able to return to his work with even greater vigor and dedication.

When we withdraw from our daily routine and seek a retreat from the pressing problems of lost and dying humanity, we need not feel guilty. In fact, the only way we can give persons our best is to regularly withdraw from them. We are so structured by God that we need periodic withdrawals to be alone with our families, ourselves, and our God.

God himself worked six days and rested on the seventh day (see Ex. 20:11). It wasn't that he took a vacation from being God. So, when we take a day off from our routine evangelism or take a vacation, it isn't that we are abandoning our role or our responsibility. On the contrary, we are preparing ourselves to do more vigorous combat with the powers of darkness.

My tendency in evangelism is to be a workaholic. But, two things I have learned. One is to take a day off each week whether I do anything else or not. The other is that a vacation pays more than it costs. One of the things which I would do differently if I could is to take more time off and spend more time alone on retreat with God, myself, and my loved ones and closest friends.

Apart from all of this, it is sobering and humbling to learn that God can get along without me, and that others can too. Withdrawals prevent us from taking ourselves too seriously. They enable us to better laugh at ourselves, and to laugh and weep more appropriately with others.

Total Withdrawal Impossible

Simultaneously with strong affirmation of withdrawals from evangelistic engagements, it must also be pointed out that total withdrawal is not always possible. Indeed, it was not possible for Jesus.

Mark's Gospel brings this fact out more clearly: "And he entered a house, and would not have any one know it; yet he could not be hid. But immediately a woman, whose little daughter was possessed by an unclean spirit, heard of him, and came and fell down at his feet" (7:24-25).

There is a world of wealth in that little phrase of Mark's, "Yet he could not be hid." One might hide a baby Moses for three months as Amram and Jochebed did (see Ex. 2:2), but hiding the Savior of the world for even a few days' retreat in the remote region of Tyre and Sidon was impossible. Can any one hide the Light of the world? Does any one seek to hide the Bread of life? Jesus can never be like a needle in a haystack!

Even when we succeed in breaking away from our regular duties, we can never completely withdraw from humanity or cut ourselves off from needy persons. There is a sense in which an evangelist is always on duty. Wherever he or she goes, he or she is to be a lighthouse for Christ, guiding human beings safely into the harbor of salvation, and preventing them from shipwrecking their lives. Witnesses take no holidays from sharing their faith.

I can tell you this about evangelism: if your heart is really in it, if you can really help persons, if you earnestly desire to be good news to others, you cannot be hid. Persons will find you out. They will seek you out. If you really give yourself to persons as did Jesus, those who receive from you will spread the word to others. Like the fictitious Listener in Taylor Caldwell's novel, you will never lack for persons beating a path to your door.[2]

Persistence

Persistence and patience pay off in evangelism. That is true of both the persistence of the petitioner and of the witness. This woman faced four obstacles in getting through to Jesus.

First, her womanhood was against her. Women in the first century, far more so than in this century, did not have the same standing in society and in religion as did men.

Second, her race was against her. Matthew calls her "a Canaanite woman" (v. 22). The Canaanites were a people of "reproach" in the Old Testament. Mark says, she was "a Greek, a Syrophoenician by birth" (Mark 7:26). Perhaps Mark calls her a Greek because she spoke the Greek language. It could be that Matthew regards Syrophoenicians as descendents of the Canaanites.[3] Clearly, she was a Gentile.

Third, the silence of Jesus seemed against her. She had come to Jesus crying out, "Have mercy on me, O Lord, Son of David; my daughter is severely possessed by a demon" (v. 22). Amazingly, Jesus "did not answer her a word" (v. 23). Isn't such stoical silence a formidable obstacle to petitioners? How would you feel if your urgent requests were met with strong silence?

A fourth obstacle faced by this Canaanite woman was the attitude of Jesus' disciples. "And his disciples came and begged him, saying, 'Send her away, for she is crying after us' " (v. 23). Not only did she meet with silence from Jesus, she met with strong negative resistance from his disciples.

Nevertheless, in spite of these four formidable obstacles, the woman got what she wanted: "O woman, great is your faith! Be it done for you as you desire" (v. 28). She didn't give up easily. Her persistence yielded rich dividends. Her daughter was instantly healed (v. 28).

If we would be as persistent with God on behalf of our loved ones and friends, would we not also be richly rewarded? L. R. Scarborough tells of a woman who prayed twenty-five years for her son's salvation; a wife who prayed forty-eight years for her husband to be saved; and how he himself prayed twelve years for the salvation of his brother.[4]

I myself prayed nine years for the salvation of one man in Virginia. It was a word from his grandchild which actually clinched his salvation, but I saw my prayers answered; and I have reason to believe that others were also praying for him.

The great prayer warrior, George Mueller, wrote:

The great point is to never give up until that answer comes. I have been praying every day for 52 years for two men, sons of a friend of my youth. They are not converted yet, but they will be! . . . The great fault of the children of God is that they do not continue in prayer—they do not go on praying; they do not persevere. If they desire anything for God's glory, they should pray until they get it.[5]

Were these two men saved? Yes. One of them became a Christian at Mueller's funeral. The other one was saved some years later.[6]

Concern About Children

There is another crown jewel in this case which we should not overlook. Parents ought to be concerned about the spiritual welfare of their children. This woman was concerned about her little daughter being possessed by a demon: "My daughter is severely possessed by a demon" (v. 22). Mark highlights the case a bit by telling us that the daughter was "little" and that she was possessed by "an unclean spirit" (see Mark 7:25).

Incidentally, we can begin to see here how fortunate we are to have two inspired records of the same case in the evangelism of Jesus. Mark's characteristic attention to details helps us to know that this was a child in the clutches of some unclean and demonic power.

God has permitted me and my wife to rear four children, two sons and two daughters. I am still concerned about what happens to my daughters and sons even though they are now grown. But when they were little and dependent upon us and others, I was even more concerned about what happened to them. Hence, I see this incident through the eyes of a parent's concern and love for his or her little ones.

How pitiful and passionate must have been this mother's cry for deliverance. She wasn't asking for herself but for her little daughter. Few things are so inspiring, or so desperate, as to see parents seeking help for their helpless children.

I see this as a case of domestic evangelism—a loving mother's concern for her dear daughter's deliverance from the powers of darkness and the kingdom of evil. It is not enough for parents to be concerned about food, shelter, education, and the physical welfare of their children. All parents who truly love their offspring should be concerned about their emotional and spiritual well-being, as was the Canaanite woman.

Our Taking the Initiative

We can also learn from this case to take the initiative in telling Jesus about our problems. This lady didn't know much about Jesus, but she knew enough to take her burdens to him.

Jesus is the world's great burden bearer. Would to God that all who are burdened and heavy laden would take the initiative and go to Jesus with their problems. Jesus can help us with any problem. No problem is too big or too small for Jesus.

There is a song which has a line which says, "Take your burden to the Lord and leave it there." We must learn to go beyond the church, beyond the Bible, and beyond the preacher to Jesus himself with our burdens! He is the final and everlasting source of deliverance and power. How I love that verse of Scripture which says, "Cast all your anxieties on him, for he cares about you" (1 Pet. 5:7).

Are you taking the initiative in telling Jesus about your problems with your children, your problems with your fellow workers, your problems with your neighbors, your problems with your finances, your problems with the lost and unreconciled whom you are seeking to reconcile to him? He invites us to take the initiative. Hear him again saying to you: "Come to me, all who labor and are heavy laden, and I will give you rest. Take my yoke upon you, and learn from me; for I am gentle and lowly in heart, and you will find rest for your souls. For my yoke is easy, and my burden is light" (Matt. 11:28-30).

Commanding Faith

Another item which we see in this case is the exhibition of topmost faith, even commanding faith in the work of evangelism. There are several kinds of faith, says L. R. Scarborough: begging faith, walking faith, living faith, conquering faith, taking faith, and commanding faith. This woman seems to have had what is called faith that commands God (see Isa. 45:11).[7]

I know this sounds audacious, and perhaps it is, but there is a sense in which she mastered Jesus with her "great" faith. Look at the text once more, "Then Jesus answered her, 'O woman, great is your faith! Be it done for you as you desire.' And her daughter was healed instantly" (v. 28).

Some of us are probably more familiar with great and grave doubts in the work of evangelism than we are with great faith. How refreshing it is for us to encounter a person whose faith is as great as was this woman's. Jesus seemed so taken with her faith that he practically gave her *carte blanche* to which she could charge whatever her heart desired.

Years ago I heard a professor of evangelism say something along these lines which stuck with me. He said, "Some of my students seem concerned to see just how little they can believe and still be called Christians. I am on the trail of such students." That was back during the "sassy sixties" when there was a shaking of the foundations of faith even among seminarians and settled pastors. Well, I wasn't one of that professor's students. But he got through to me. He was on my trail, too, and didn't know it.

I want for myself and for my students, for those on my evangelism potential list, and for my family and friends, the kind of faith which the Canaanite woman possessed. Don't you? We have this word from him to whom has been committed "all authority in heaven and on earth" (see Matt. 28:18): "Truly, I say to you, if you have faith and never doubt, you will not only do what has been done to the fig tree, but even if you say to this mountain, 'Be taken up and cast into the sea,' it will be done. And whatever you ask in prayer, you will receive, if you have faith" (Matt. 21:21-22). "Hyperbole," you say? Perhaps so. But, then, on the other hand maybe there is simply a scarcity of Canaanites in our world!

The Diabolical Nature of Sin

The diabolical nature of sin and evil may be seen in this case. Sin will enter into, and master and control a little girl and break a mother's heart. It will wreck our home, dig our graves, damn our destiny, dethrone God, and wreck the universe. Sin is no respecter of persons. Indeed, "the wages of sin is death" (Rom. 6:23).

A Word of Caution

This case bespeaks a word of caution to Christian workers. Hear again with the ears of the heart: "And his disciples came and begged him, saying, 'Send her away, for she is crying after us' " (v. 23). God forbid that we shall stand in the way of others who would come to Jesus. Let us not want Jesus so much for ourselves that we forget he came for others too!

Are not the disciples to *bring* others to Jesus rather than to *ban* them from him? Should not his disciples offer themselves as *stepping-stones* on the path to Jesus rather than becoming *stumbling blocks*? Does our Lord ever need to be protected from brokenhearted mothers? Where did we ever get the idea that Jesus needed us as a bodyguard, or a secret service, to prevent petitioners from seeing him and speaking face-to-face with him?

Then, there is another angle from which to view this sorry spectacle of his disciples keeping a poor lady from the Savior. She may have been "bugging" them so pestiferously that they "begged him" (v. 23) for relief from her. What a sight! One Canaanite woman, with a broken heart and a demon-possessed daughter, intimidates twelve of the Master's men!

Mark makes it clear that the daughter was at home. She did not accompany her mother (see Mark 7:29-30). So, my guess is that this woman had fire in her bones and steel in her determination. The disciples seemed afraid of her, and well might they be. Let us thank God that some sinners are so bent on getting to Jesus that not even the twelve apostles can stop them. Yet, how sad it is that some persons who really need to get to Jesus have to almost run over certain Christian disciples in order to get to him.

The Role of a Midwife in Evangelism

Paul tells us that "there is one mediator between God and men, the man Christ Jesus, who gave himself as a ransom for all" (1 Tim. 2:5-6). Strictly speaking, then, the *one* mediator is the man Christ Jesus. Perhaps our role with the mediator in evangelization is more that of a midwife. We are God's midwives assisting in the new birth of his sons and daughters.

We can't conceive children of God. That is the work of the Spirit. But we can and must assist with the birthing process. Hence, while God alone can furnish the mediator, we are honored to be the midwives, and the spiritual obstetricians and pediatricians in the Kingdom's nursery.

What a beautiful picture then may be seen in this case. The girl's own mother becomes her midwife in getting Jesus to heal her. It would be great if parents would become evangelistic midwives in the evangelization of their children.

Use of Humor

We may see in this case an example of Jesus using humor in evangelism. Some have suggested that Jesus playfully used the diminutive word for dogs, *kunaria,* meaning "doggies" or "puppies," thus indicating that he really did not despise foreigners as did some other Jews.[8]

The relevant verses are Matthew 15:24-27, and especially verses 26 and 27. Those latter two verses read: "And he answered, 'It is not fair to take the children's bread and throw it to the dogs.' She said, 'Yes, Lord, yet even the dogs eat the crumbs that fall from their masters' table.' " I believe that this is humorous banter in which both Jesus and the woman engage. "That Jesus was indulging in this kind of banter about racial and national differences," says Elton Trueblood, "is the only logical alternative to the insufferable hypothesis that He was being intentionally chauvinistic and rude."[9]

This may well be the clearest case of the use of humor in the evangelism of Jesus. Whatever the explanation for such language, we can be sure that our Lord was no racist and that he was not intentionally rude or chauvinistic.

Role of Silence

That brings me to the final point which I should like to make in conjunction with this case. Earlier, I listed the initial silence of Jesus as a possible obstacle to the woman. The other side of silence is that it can play a positive role in our evangelizing.

Psalm 46:10 says, "Be still, and know that I am God." There are times when silence in evangelism is yellow and cowardly. However, there are other times when silence in evangelism can be yellow and golden and good.

Our Lord was no coward. His silence was golden (v. 23). Some of us may need to learn when to speak and when to shut up. If we remain silent when we ought to speak, we play the coward. However, if we answer with a torrent of words when we ought to hold our peace, we play the fool.

I used to get uptight during all silences in evangelistic encounters. Through experience I have learned that even in this work of reconciliation, when we share "the message of reconciliation" (see 2 Cor. 5:19), as Ecclesiastes says, "There is . . . a time to keep silence, and a time to speak" (Eccl. 3:1,7b).

Notes

1. L. R. Scarborough, *How Jesus Won Men* (Grand Rapids: Baker Book House, 1972 reprint), p. 124.

2. See Taylor Caldwell, *The Listener* (Garden City, NY: Doubleday & Co., Inc., 1960).

3. See Sherman E. Johnson, "The Gospel According to St. Matthew: Introduction and Exegesis," in *The Interpreter's Bible,* Vol. VII (New York: Abingdon Press, 1951), pp. 441-42.

4. See Scarborough, *How Jesus Won Men,* pp. 126-27.

5. Quoted by Jim Peterson, *Evangelism As a Life-style* (Colorado Springs, CO: Navpress, 1980), p. 142.

6. See ibid., p. 142.

7. See Scarborough, *How Jesus Won Men,* pp. 128-29.

8. See Sherman E. Johnson, "The Gospel According to St. Matthew: Introduction and Exegesis," *The Interpreter's Bible,* Vol. VII (New York: Abingdon Press, 1951), p. 442.

9. See Elton Trueblood, *The Humor of Christ* (New York: Harper & Row, Publishers, 1964), p. 123.

14

The Centurion
Whose Slave Was Ill

Isaiah 49:12-13; Luke 7:1-10

Let us now examine the case of the centurion whose slave was ill. I shall follow primarily the text of Luke 7:1-10. Matthew 8:5-13 is a New Testament parallel which differs significantly in that the centurion himself comes to Jesus with his request. John 4:46-54 is also somewhat comparable. This is another of the cases which centers around a physical healing.

Universality and Particularity

We can see both the universality and the particularity of Jesus in this case. Jesus was a Jew, but he was also the Savior of the world. Probably the centurion was a Roman. Luke 7:9 presupposes, and Luke 7:5 implies, that the centurion was a non-Jew.

The centurion sent some "elders of the Jews" (see v. 3) to petition Jesus on his behalf. However, the request was for the healing of the centurion's slave. The word *slave* is used throughout, except in verse 7 where he is called a servant. Matthew 8:11-12 brings out the universality of Jesus more clearly: "I tell you, many will come from east and west and sit at table with Abraham, Isaac, and Jacob in the kingdom of heaven, while the sons of the kingdom will be thrown into the outer darkness; there men will weep and gnash their teeth."

The case shows that Jesus, a Jew who was petitioned by Jewish elders, was also concerned about a Roman centurion *and* a sick slave. Whatever your daily work may be, Jesus Christ is concerned about you. He takes notice of you. He is a Savior who ministers without regard to distinctions such as race, national origin, economic worth, or social standing. Jesus is an equal opportunity Savior. He is indeed "the Savior of the world" as the Samaritans said in John 4:42.

That chorus which we teach our little children is true: "Red and yellow, black and white, they are precious in His sight." What other Savior is as concerned for the salvation of a slave as he is for the salvation of a master?

Worthiness

The appeal which the elders made to Jesus was based on the centurion's worthiness, that is, his nationalism and his philanthropy. "And when they came to Jesus, they besought him earnestly, saying, 'He is worthy to have you do this for him, for he loves our nation, and he built us our synagogue' " (vv. 4-5).

Jesus may have responded to their appeal not so much out of their testimony as out of his compassion. At any rate, this is a strange military man. The Jewish elders said, "He is worthy" (v. 4). Whereas, the centurion himself said, "I am not worthy to have you come under my roof" (v. 6).

One can hardly escape the conclusion that Luke wished to highlight the fact that one is never worthy of the grace of God. Mark carefully the contrast between the way the Jewish elders see the centurion and the way he sees himself. Those who would enter into the presence of God should be aware of their own unworthiness.

Four facts stand out about this centurion. First, he was one Roman who apparently had wide and deep sympathies with the Jewish nation. The Jewish elders said, "He loves our nation" (v. 5). Second, he was a generous man. His philanthropy had expressed itself tangibly: "He built us our synagogue" (v. 5).

Third, the man was sensitive to Jewish customs. He was aware that Jews were not supposed to enter the home of a Gentile. That respect led him to say, "I am not worthy to have you come under my roof" (v. 6). Fourth, the centurion recognized his own unworthiness, in spite of the testimony to his worthiness (see vv. 4-5).

Our righteousness is but as filthy rags in God's sight. None of us is worthy of what God does for us. Only the Lamb of God "is worthy to open the scroll and break its seals" (Rev. 5:2). We make a big mistake if we think one has to be worthy before he or she can receive the compassion and the cure of the Savior of the world.

John 3:16 is the world's greatest love story. It is written, as S. M. Lockridge says, in the key of "Be"; that is, "Be saved." This is the anthem of redemption. You start out saying it, and you end up singing it.

I'm not going to heaven because I'm a Baptist. If I believed that, I'd strap a baptistry to my back. I'm going to heaven because one day my heart was broken; my life was miserable; I was so unhappy that I felt like I was going to die. Then I did what my Sunday School teacher and my foster parents told me to do. I confessed my sins to God. I asked God to help me. As best I knew how, I placed my life into the hands of Jesus. That's the reason I expect to go to heaven when I die.

I seem to recall a hymn which has a line or two something like this:

> In my hand no price I bring;
> Simply to Thy cross I cling.

Well might we reflect upon the meaning of justice, mercy, and grace in conjunction with our unworthiness, or the lack of it. Justice is when we get what we deserve from God. Mercy is when God does not give us what we deserve. Grace is when God gives us what we do not deserve.

Authority and Obedience

Authority and obedience are coupled together in evangelism. That is what we may infer from the words of verses 7-8: "But say the word, and let my servant be healed. For I am a man set under authority, with soldiers under me: and I say to one, 'Go,' and he goes; and to another, 'Come,' and he comes; and to my slave, 'Do this,' and he does it."

Those who have authority practice obedience. Those who are obedient have authority. The path to authority in evangelism is that of obedience.

Remember how Jesus coupled authority and the Great Commission in Matthew 28:16-20. "All authority in heaven and on earth has been given to me. Go therefore and make disciples of all nations" (vv. 18-19). To him who was obedient unto death was given all authority.

This centurion projected his own authority to Jesus. Only he seemed to project it on a higher level. He seemed to know that Jesus was Lord, and acted accordingly.

The "keys of the kingdom of heaven" (see Matt. 16:19) are given not just to Simon Peter, but to all who make and obey the great confession, "You are the Christ, the Son of the living God" (Matt. 16:16). Those keys represent authority to bind and to loose (see Matt. 16:19). Our custom of a mayor presenting to a distinguished guest the key to the city may continue to represent the symbolical power of keys.

The centurion recognized that there was an authority greater than his, and greater than Rome's. All who would have authority must themselves obey a higher authority.

Have you ever had a eureka experience? *Eureka* means, "I found it." It is an experience which comes like a flash of lightning. Suddenly, almost in the twinkle of an eye, an insight is gained or something falls into place for us. Well, I had one of those eureka experiences with this case. God showed me something about authority and obedience. If you would have power with God and power with people, obey God with all your heart and serve your fellowmen as did Jesus.

Hit-and-run evangelism doesn't have much authority because it may not cost as much in obedience. We should become more conscious of the dangers of hit-and-run evangelism. That kind of evangelism ought to be as illegal as hit-and-run driving.

Vicarious Faith

See also here the role of vicarious faith in evangelism. The vicarious faith of the centurion, exercised in Jesus the Christ, resulted in the healing of his slave. Jesus said, "I tell you, not even in Israel have I found such faith" (v. 9).

Such faith seems to inspire faith. Jesus said to the centurion, according to Matthew's account, "Go; be it done for you as you have believed" (8:13). Matthew then comments, "And the servant was healed at that very moment" (8:13).

Intercession for others may be our greatest ministry in evangelism. What does this kind of vicarious faith imply for a ministry of prayer in evangelism? The way we intercede with God on behalf of others may be the greatest index of devotion in our work.

There is a sense in which each of us is the product of someone else's faith. Even in the ultimate sense, we are the fruit of Christ's own intercession. He believed for us when we could not, or would not, believe for ourselves.

The blessings which come to those who intercede for others are great indeed. They transcend distance, break down barriers, and move mountains as it were.

The Help of Others

Seldom does one come to Christ without the aid of others. Particularly is this true of those who are physically incapacitated. Fix your eyes and mind upon the network of others who put the sick slave in touch with the healing power of the Savior.

First and foremost, there was the slave's master, the centurion. If I were a slave, I think I should prefer a master like that. Wouldn't you?

Second, there were the elders of the Jews. When the centurion heard of Jesus, he enlisted the help of the Jewish elders (see vv. 2-3). The slave was sick to the point of death. The centurion was desperate. Perhaps he thought the Jewish elders would carry more weight with Jesus, a Jew.

Third, were the friends of the centurion. "When he was not far from the house, the centurion sent friends to him, 'Lord, do not trouble yourself . . . ' " (v. 6). Hence, we see a second kind of buffer which the centurion used on behalf of his dear slave.

Let me cite you a true story of how others helped a whole tribe come to Christ. A remarkable people movement seems to have happened in 1981 among the so-called tribe of Mindanao, the Manobos. Southern Baptist missionary Chuck Morris saw 125 persons accept Christ in fourteen days.

Morris says he was the first white man to reach the place where the lost tribe lived. It took him three days to walk thirty miles to reach Tumagok. "I had forded rivers, balanced on logs and walked two half-inch cables 70 feet above a crocodile infested river," says Morris. "I had

burrowed through 10-foot-high jungle grass, slid down 45-degree
mountain slopes and crept through dark jungles."

The female leader of the primitive religion of the Manobos was an
elderly woman who prayed for her tribe to come down the mountain
and hear Morris preach the message about Jesus Christ. This story is so
unusual that I shall from this point on let the missionary relate it in his
own words:

Morning light revealed the tribe flowing down the mountain, some having
walked two hours. Soon the little hut was packed with 35 adults and three times
that many children and young people.

For one and one-half hours I told them about Jesus, over and over again the
same story. When I invited them to accept Christ the old woman was the first to
stand.

An 80-year-old man who was hearing the news for the first time, stood to say,
"Put my name down as one who accepts." A division chief who walked six
miles to hear, believed. Another 84-year-old chief said, "We have not known.
We now believe. I will be baptized. I will give a piece of land for a church site."

I asked those who had stood making decisions to sit down and I carefully
explained the meaning of what they were doing. I taught them about baptism
and the need to witness their belief about Jesus. Then I went to the river. Soon
25 adults and older young people had streamed down the hill to witness their
faith by baptism.

Like chickens flocking for food they came; they heard; they believed; they
went away satisfied. In 14 days, 125 people accepted Christ.

At the last service, the translator said to the people, "We have been called the
lost tribe of Mindanao. This can't be said any longer. Since Brother Morris has
brought the gospel to our tribe God has found us."

As I turned to start the long walk out of the mountains, the old woman
crossed her arms, took both my hands in hers and raised her hands toward
heaven in an act of benediction and prayer for me. Taking my hands again, she
kissed them, and weeping said, "You have become my brother."[1]

The Unusual

Do we not also behold the unusual in evangelism in this case? To
begin with, a centurion was an unusual man. He was no ordinary man.
Centurions were equivalents to what we call company sergeants major.
They were the backbone of the Roman army. Always whenever they
are mentioned in the New Testament, they are spoken of well.[2]

But, more than that, this centurion was unusual in other important respects. He was a very religious man. Here was a military man who was genuinely pious and God-fearing.

This centurion was also unusual in his attitude toward the Jewish people, toward his slave, and toward himself. Evidently he harbored no racial prejudice toward Jews; believed that his ill slave was a human being with rights and privileges; and exercised genuine humility in his opinion of himself.

No wonder Jesus was so taken with this man. He sounds like a very decent human being. Rarely do we meet such men and women in our evangelization.

More frequently than we meet unusual persons in our evangelizing, do we see unusual things happening to unusual persons. For example, George Wallace was a noted segregationist during his political heyday. However, when Wallace was struck down by an assassin's bullet, he began to reorient his life and his values. Now, he says groups who use the Bible to defend racism are "deadly wrong." Wallace added, "There is nothing in the Bible to indicate you can get in heaven by hating anyone because of race, color, creed, or national origin."

Wallace says the shooting taught him the frailty of human life. "One moment you are in perfectly good health and in the twinkling of an eye you can be dead . . . or paralyzed," he said.[3]

Healing at a Distance

The centurion's servant is an example of one who was healed at a distance. The only other such example in the three Gospels of Matthew, Mark, and Luke is that of the Canaanite woman (see Matt. 15:21-28). The possible parallel in John 4:46-54 also presents a healing at quite a distance.

Therefore, the healing word of Jesus (see Matt. 8:13) is effectual at a distance. Jesus doesn't have to be present at the actual point of need in order for his word to have power.

It is only one step beyond that for us to observe that the power of the saving word of Jesus does not require his physical presence. Jesus can also heal us and save us at a distance.

Evangelism is a life-and-death matter. Jesus makes all the difference in the world. That is what evangelism is all about.

A Time to Remember

Matthew's account of this case strikes a note about time in connection with evangelism: "And the servant was healed at that very moment" (Matt. 8:13). Somehow I see that as the evangelist's way of telling us that some times are worth remembering—such as the time we were healed from our sins and saved from our evil deeds.

Baseball fans have followed the career of Darrell Porter with keen interest. In 1980 Porter left spring camp for six weeks of agony in Arizona at a drug and alcohol rehabilitation center. He made a comeback but left the Kansas City Royals and joined the Saint Louis Cardinals in 1981.

Someone asked Porter when he had his last drink. He thought for a moment and then replied, "It'll be thirteen months on the nose this Sunday." The interrogator said, "You remember the date?" Porter answered tersely, "Wouldn't you? That was the most important day of my whole life. If I hadn't stopped, just think where I'd be now."[4]

When we get liberated from some killing habit, or set free from some evil monster, that's a day worth remembering. One aspect of salvation is deliverance from all tyrannies. As the psalmist wrote: "Deliverance belongs to the Lord" (3:8). A word from the Lord to all who are in bondage to alcohol, drugs, or any other slavemaster of this world is: "I bring near my deliverance, it is not far off" (Isa. 46:13).

Notes

1. See Chuck Morris, "Lost Mindanao Tribe Says 'God Found Us,' " *The WORD and WAY,* Vol. 118, No. 15, April 9, 1981, p. 11. Used by permission.

2. See William Barclay, *The Gospel of Luke* (Edinburgh: The Saint Andrew Press, 3rd. ed., 1956), p. 82.

3. See "Using the Bible to Defend Racism Is 'Deadly Wrong' Says Wallace," *The WORD and WAY,* Vol. 118, No. 16, April 16, 1981, p. 3.

4. See Jay Mariotti, "Irony: Porter Toils for Busch," *The Detroit News,* April 11, 1981, p. 3-B.

15

The Two Thieves

Psalm 22:1-8; Luke 23:32-47

Let us look now at the case of two thieves as presented in Luke 23:32-47. You will find very brief New Testament parallels in Mark 15:32 and Matthew 27:44. However, only Luke in his "Gospel to the outcasts" records the story of one thief's conversion at the eleventh hour. The heart of the case may be seen in Luke 23:39-43.

Criminals Can Be Saved

Criminals can be saved. That is one of the shining truths presented by this case. Moses was a criminal, and he was saved. He murdered an Egyptian soldier and buried his body in the sand. The Scripture says of Moses, "He looked this way and that, and seeing no one he killed the Egyptian and hid him in the sand" (Ex. 2:12). Yet, God mightily used Moses as his lawgiver and as the leader of the nation Israel. God was not done with Moses even though he had killed a man. Moses even appeared in the transfiguration along with Elijah and Jesus (see Matt. 17:1-8).

Saul of Tarsus was also a criminal, but God saved him and made him Paul the apostle to the Gentiles. When Stephen was stoned, "The witnesses laid down their garments at the feet of a young man named Saul" (Acts 7:58). The Scripture says, "Saul was consenting to his death" (Acts 8:1). Later in that same place we are told that "Saul laid waste the church" (Acts 8:3). Yet, God turned this murderer into a missionary, this persecutor of the church into a preacher of Christ Jesus.

This criminal who was hanged alongside the Christ said of himself and the other thief, "We are receiving the due reward of our deeds" (v. 41). He knew he deserved death, but Jesus gave him eternal life.

Some of us were once criminals. Now we are the sons and daughters of the King. We were once afar off, but the death of Christ has brought us close to God. We were nobodies; but God made us somebodies.

Perhaps you have committed some crime. You may have covered your tracks well. Indeed, no one else may even know of your crime. God knows, because he knows the number of hairs on your head. He sees and knows all. He can see in the dark as well as in the daylight.

An Associated Press report from Trenton, New Jersey, told about a burglary suspect who eluded arrest by hiding in a chimney. The problem was that he slipped and fell down the chimney and was stuck for six days in total darkness and soot. Fire fighters had to dismantle the chimney in order to get him out![1] Be sure your sins will find you out.

God knows your dreadful, shameful deeds. But he loves you still. He wants to forgive you and help you. He wants to heal you and lighten your burdens.

One of my favorite verses in the Bible is Romans 8:28: "We know that in everything God works for good with those who love him, who are called according to his purpose." We see this providential working together for good even in the moral and ethical fiasco of Watergate. Charles Colson, for example, one of the most noted Watergate criminals, has been converted to Jesus Christ. Moreover, Colson the prisoner was called by God into a fruitful ministry to prisoners and their families. His ministry moved into a new headquarters building in 1980 and has expanded into Canada.[2]

You can be saved in spite of all your crimes. All the powers of darkness can't keep Jesus from saving you right now, if you will trust in him and turn your life over to him. Do not the Scriptures say, "The blood of Jesus his Son cleanses us from all sin" (1 John 1:7)?

Choice on Deathbed

It is possible, according to this case, for one to be saved on his or her deathbed. So long as there is life, there is hope. Let me enlarge just a bit on that crucial truth. While this is the only instance of a deathbed conversion in the Gospels, it did happen, and it can happen again. So long as there is physical life, there is hope of eternal life..

Salvation is in the ultimate analysis instantaneous. At least that appears to be so from our present perspective. The only thing necessary for salvation, strictly speaking, is turning from sin and trusting in Christ alone to save. Baptism, church membership, prayer and Bible study, these—and more—are needed in Christian obedience, but they are not the point of entrance into the kingdom of God.

The dying, repentant thief said, "Jesus, remember me when you come in your kingdom" (v. 42). Evidently, this thief believed the inscription over the cross of Christ, "This is the King of the Jews" (v. 38). My guess is that he believed even more than that. Be that as it may, our Lord said to this "eleventh-hour" disciple,. "Truly, I say to you, today you will be with me in Paradise" (v. 43).

You may have waited a long time. You may have put it off and procrastinated time and time again. You might even feel that you have sinned away your day of grace. But this case reminds us that now is not too late. It's seldom too late to get right with God. God's supply of grace is inexhaustible. Let us take to heart what the Lord said to his servant, Paul: "My grace is sufficient for you, for my power is made perfect in weakness" (2 Cor. 12:9).

The Role of Confession

Confession also has a role to play in evangelism. The case of the two thieves seems to lift that up. We may see a type of confession in the rebuke of the penitent thief, "Do you not fear God, since you are under the same sentence of condemnation? And we indeed justly; for we are receiving the due reward of our deeds; but this man has done nothing wrong" (vv. 40-41).

The role of confession is accentuated by the centurion. "Now when the centurion saw what had taken place, he praised God, and said, 'Certainly this man was innocent!' " (v. 47). Matthew's account has the centurion and those who were with him to confess, "Truly this was the Son of God!" (Matt. 27:54).

What kind of confession should we look for in our evangelizing? We should look for confession of sin. Like the tax collector about whom Jesus told, we may listen to hear persons say, "God be merciful to me a sinner" (Luke 18:13). Also, we may look for persons to confess that Jesus is Lord.

Centrality of the Cross

The cross is central in evangelism. That is another truth which deserves being highlighted in this case. Jesus was crucified between two thieves. His cross is forever in the center of all crosses. All evangelism begins at the cross or eventually ends at the cross. Charles H. Spurgeon, the great preacher who was never ordained, said, "I take a text and then head straight toward the cross."

For about sixteen years a five- by four-foot Salvador Dali painting on the crucifixion hung on the dining room wall of Rikers Island Jail in New York state. A Manhattan art dealer valued the painting at $75,000 to $100,000. The moment the warden discovered its value, down came the picture from the wall. It was placed in the warden's office for safekeeping.[3] Isn't it interesting how we don't always recognize the values of certain treasures all around us?

There is a footnote to this story about an original Salvador Dali. The prison officials have decided to place it back in the mess hall where it hung unmolested for sixteen years. Perhaps the crucifixion will do the prisoners more good this way than it would have had the picture been turned into cash.[4]

Paul, in what is probably a reference to Jeremiah 9:23-24, exclaimed: "But far be it from me to glory except in the cross of our Lord Jesus Christ, by which the world has been crucified to me, and I to the world" (Gal. 6:14). The cross was certainly central in the great apostle's preaching. One may boast in the cross because he or she is then glorying in what God has done for the reconciliation of the world.

Calvary requires persons to choose. The ground around the cross is anything but neutral. Neutral, you cannot be. God took his stand on that ground, and so must you and I, if we would be messengers of the cross.

The Comfort of Heaven

Along with the good confession comes the comfort of the afterlife and of heaven. Jesus said to the dying man, "Today you will be with me in Paradise" (v. 43). The thought of heaven is especially precious in times of death. A dying person often longs to hear the promises of heaven. The assurance of Christ's presence when we walk through the valley of the shadow of death is worth more than all the gold at Fort Knox.

Nevertheless, our motivation for righteous living and a life-style of holiness does not arise so much from our belief in heaven or in hell as it does from our belief in God. "Father, into thy hands I commit my spirit" (v. 46).

Jonathan Edwards resolved that he would live uprightly regardless of whether he would spend eternity in heaven or hell. His resolution number 50, dated July 5, 1723, reads: "That I will act so, as I think I shall judge would have been best, and most prudent, when I come into the future world." Three days later, on July 8, 1723, Edwards wrote a resolution numbered 51, which said: "That I will act so, in every respect, as I think I shall wish I had done, if I should at last be damned."[5]

Cynicism

Occasionally we meet with cynicism in our evangelizing. It was present in this case. "One of the criminals who were hanged railed at him, saying, 'Are you not the Christ? Save yourself and us!' " (v. 39).

See how the cynicism comes from the unrepentant. There is none from Jesus; and should be none from his witnesses. Cynicism is always one way in evangelization. It is from the other side toward us. The smallest pore of a Christian's skin should never harbor so much as one-thousandth of an ounce of cynicism. There is absolutely no legitimate place for cynicism in Christian evangelism. The cynic will be as ineffective as a dodo in evangelism.

I hasten to add, however, that you and I may increasingly be faced with more cynics than we have seen since the 1960s. Some observers, for example, are now talking about "Europe's lost generation." Throughout Western Europe teenage unemployment has soared. Forty percent of jobless persons in the common market are under age twenty-five. Housing is a real problem. So are alcoholism, drug abuse, and suicide. "Europe's dead-end kids have lost faith in the future. They share no political commitment, no heroes, no ideology—and, often, no enthusiasm for solutions." Their philosophy is strikingly like the words on graffiti in West Berlin, "Self, not society."[6] Corresponding signs may also be seen in North America.

Jesus gives us an example in how to deal with cynicism. When he was reviled, he reviled not in turn. Stony silence from Jesus, he uttered not a word. But see how he let the believing thief rebuke the unbelieving one (vv. 40-41). Frequently, others will deal appropriately with cynicism. Don't you agree that this man's partner in crime dealt quite adequately with his friend's cynicism?

The Curtain

Immediately following the word of Christ about Paradise a curtain of darkness engulfed the earth (see v. 44). Simultaneously, the curtain of the Temple was torn in two (see v. 45). The darkness lasted three hours. Was not that literal darkness symbolical of the diabolical darkness of sin and evil which nailed the Christ to the cross?

That curtain which separated the holy place from the holy of holies was ripped in two, "from top to bottom" as Matthew says (see Matt. 27:51). That means it could not have been done by human hands. This renting of the veil opened up the holy of holies to all persons. Now, all persons can come directly to God without the mediation of some earthly priest.

No one will ever be able to put that curtain back into place again because of what Christ wrought for us on the cross. Nevertheless, another kind of curtain will fall on this world one day. Part of what it means to say that history is linear is that we are moving from the creation to the judgment. God himself will let down the curtain which ends history and consummates all things. We know not when that hour will come. The best advice we can give may be the words of our Lord, "Work . . . while it is day; night comes, when no one can work" (John 9:4).

Jesus said, "The fields are already white for harvest" (John 4:35). When the wheat turns white, it is already overripe. It begins to fall out of the husks and away from the stalk. How much longer God will give us to reap and sow we do not know. Therefore, let us labor the more diligently before that last curtain falls and we shall be able to work no more in this eon.

The Evangelistic Calling

One final note concerning the evangelistic calling may be uttered. Evangelism was a passion with Jesus. He witnessed to a man even at the very end of his earthly life. Jesus came "preaching the gospel of God" (Mark 1:14) and he died preaching the same good news. Nothing, not even his own death, would keep him from his Father's business.

Those of us who have a calling from God can do no less. The servant is never greater than his or her master. We are never released from our calling to evangelize, not even in the face of our own death. What the Lord of the church said to Smyrna, he says to us all, "Be faithful unto death, and I will give you the crown of life" (Rev. 2:10).

Legend has it that the New Zealand kiwi lost its ability to fly through disuse of its wings. Is it possible that we shall lose our ability to evangelize by failing to evangelize when God gives us an opportunity? Our Lord, the perfect model evangelist, was presented an opportunity to evangelize while he was nailed to a cross. He seized that opportunity like he did all others.

Polycarp (70-156) was one of the earliest Christian martyrs. He was burned at stake when he was eighty-six years old. When asked to denounce Christ and to take an oath to Caesar, Polycarp said: "I have served him (Christ) eighty-six years, and he never did me any wrong. How can I blaspheme the King who saved me?" What a witness!

Evangelism is wherever we want to find it. Jesus found it on a cruel cross; Polycarp found it on a fiery stake. Where will you and I find it?

Notes

1. See "Foiled by a Chimney," *The Kansas City Times,* April 21, 1981, p. A-3.

2. See the news report on this in *Christianity Today,* XXIV, No. 21, Dec. 12, 1980, p. 61.

3. See "Dali Painting Found on Prison Wall," *The Kansas City Times,* March 24, 1981, p. A-7.

4. See Hugh A. Mulligan, "Dali's Art Remains in Jail as Special Gift to Prisoners," *The Kansas City Star,* April 5, 1981, p. D-3.

5. Quoted by Patrick Henry in "The Last Word," *The Christian Century,* XCVIII, No. 12, April 8, 1981, p. 387.

6. See "Europe's Dead-End Kids," *Newsweek,* April 27, 1981, pp. 52,57.